Dear Anthony _____ ura

We are _____

Cleveland Co _____ because
we have been loved,
supported and encouraged
by good friends like you.
We are blessed by your
friendship.

Love,

Jim · MaryLou

CLEVELAND
COUPLES

CLEVELAND C⊕UPLES

40 Inspiring Stories of Love & Commitment

KATHY DAWSON

Photographs by Caydie Heller

GRAY & COMPANY, PUBLISHERS • CLEVELAND

To the memory of my cousin, Susan Small,
whose life was one of my life's greatest joys.
Through her paintings and loving spirit,
she is with me always.

Gray & Company, Publishers
1588 E. 40th St.
Cleveland, OH 44103
www.grayco.com

Library of Congress Cataloging-in-Publication Data
Dawson, Kathy.
Cleveland Couples: 40 Inspiring Stories of Love & Commitment.
p. cm.
ISBN 1-886228-82-5
1. Marriage-Ohio-Cleveland-Case studies. 2. Couples-Ohio-
Cleveland-Case studies. I. Title.
HQ557.C54D38 2004
306.81'09771'32-dc22   2003024923

Printed in the United States of America
First Printing

Contents

Introduction

When a man and a woman are wed, they create a life force no less vibrant, wondrous, and full of possibilities than that of a newborn baby. That life force is called a marriage. Although it is often referred to as an institution or a state, it is much more than a framework or structure. A marriage is a living, breathing entity, separate from the two people who say "I do."

Every marriage has a story. As a relationship coach and author on the topic of marriage and relationships, I have heard innumerable stories, the themes of which are often pain and despair. I know exactly what makes men and women get divorced, remarry, and get divorced again. Although much can be learned from people's mistakes, I think more can be learned from people's successes.

A successful marriage is a victory, and one that needs to be spotlighted. For every couple that struggles to celebrate their first, twenty-third, or fifty-fifth wedding anniversary, there is a couple that doesn't struggle to celebrate their first, twenty-third, or fifty-fifth wedding anniversary.

This book shines a spotlight on 40 Cleveland couples whose stories of commitment are also stories of power—transformative power. You will read about the lives of men and women from varying professions and ethnic backgrounds. Some husbands and wives are high-profile Cleveland couples you will recognize instantly. Others, although not as recognizable, share stories no less poignant and inspirational.

When I first began this project, I had a short list of couples I wanted to include in the book. After my first few interviews, I noticed that the book was beginning to take on a life of its own. The search for couples, which began in a rather narrow and targeted fashion, became broader and more far reaching the more men and women I interviewed, for they would inevitably say, "We know a perfect couple for your book!" Before I knew it, one couple would lead to another couple who would lead to another couple and so on, until I had interviewed and written the stories of 40 couples throughout the entire Cleveland metropolitan area.

Before you dive into the lives of these interesting people, let me dispel any notion that the stories in this book are all sugar and spice and nothing but nice. Yes, you will read of couples who have romanced each other, proposed in unorthodox ways, and who have fun together. But, you will also read about the "dark side" to a successful marriage.

What you will learn from this book, whether you are on the cusp of getting divorced or whether divorce is the furthest thing from your mind, is that you and your partner are not alone. There isn't a happily married couple walking this planet that hasn't paid their dues. Call them challenges, struggles, issues, or plain old-fashioned problems, all successful marriages have had them. In fact, I can say with confidence that it is *because* of the problems that these marriages have not only survived, but have thrived.

To me, marriage is like a baseball glove. It's only when it has caught some line drives, been stretched out over time, and has become weathered that it performs at its peak. When a player first puts his or her hand into the glove, the glove feels stiff and almost immoveable. With every fastball, pop fly, or hard-hit grounder that lands in it, the glove bends, softens, and widens until it can catch just about anything that's thrown its way. It's the same with a marriage.

Although there is no secret formula for marital success or

magic bullet a couple can take to insure they will have a fruitful, lifelong relationship, there are certain common denominators that appear in successful marriages.

One of the similarities between the couples in this book is that many of the husbands and wives have opposite personalities and temperaments. Where one is emotional and verbal, the other is logical and less talkative. Where one is a worrier or a driven, type-A personality, the other is relaxed and carefree. It isn't just the couple's awareness of their different personalities that contributes to their winning relationship—it's their gratitude for those differences. Rather than try to mold their partner into a carbon copy of themselves, these men and women celebrate the balance that their opposite qualities create.

A joint passion or vision seems to be a repeating theme in many of the stories. In some cases, the couple's mission is a global one. In other cases, it is personal. Whether the husband and wife are committed to peace and justice, or to using their musical, theatrical, or cooking talents, they share a passion. Driven toward the same goal, they work together to achieve it.

Spirituality, religious belief, and faith were also common threads running throughout many of the stories in this book. The couples who felt that faith made their marriage strong and resilient talked about the power of prayer in their lives. Whether or not the husbands and wives practiced the same religion, they couldn't deny the positive impact their own personal belief in God had on their marriage.

The effect of humor on a marriage appears in many of the stories. Through some of the most challenging situations, these couples somehow found reasons to laugh. Being lighthearted and playful has been paramount to their success as a couple.

Of the steps the couples in this book have taken to insure the success of their marriage, one stands out more than any other. During the times when their relationships were stressed and strained, many of these couples didn't hesitate to reach out for help. Some sought professional counseling. Others became involved in Marriage Encounter or a marriage retreat. Regardless of what outside resource they used, they all said the same thing: Number one, they weren't ashamed of getting help; and number two, they'd do it again if they had to.

The couples who sought professional help for their relationship share a characteristic with the rest of the couples in this book. That characteristic is courage. With each interview, I walked away feeling a wealth of gratitude as well as admiration for the men and women who took a leap of faith and told their story. For a couple to share with me the evolution of their relationship, their personal, romantic memories, and their private struggles, put them in a vulnerable position. Regardless, these couples were generous with their hearts and forthcoming with their memories. I had the privilege of being shown some of their most precious mementos, ranging from seashells to bulls' horns, from cherished photos to private poetry. Every item held extraordinary significance.

As you enter the private world of the couples in this book, my hope is that you step into their lives with a sense of respect and humility. Sit back, relax, and accept the gift they have given you—the gift of their story.

CLEVELAND
COUPLES

A Match Made in Salt Water

ROGER & STEFANI SCHAEFER

The event was a wedding dinner. The place was La Dolce Vita restaurant in Little Italy. Stefani Schaefer was sitting with family and friends of the bride and groom when she looked up to see the man of her dreams walk through the door.

"We instantly locked eyes," remembers Stefani. "That moment was so dramatic, right out of a movie. I could have sworn music started playing and I saw a halo around his head. Everything was in slow motion. We spent the rest of the evening exchanging glances and flirting. I remember thinking, *It's not like me to go talk to a guy I don't know,* but that whole weekend I was mad at myself for letting him leave the restaurant without introducing myself."

For Stefani Schaefer to meet her future husband, Roger, in such a theatrical manner fit in with the theme for most of her life up to that point. One of two children, she was raised in a family of entertainers. She and her brother spent much of their childhood touring with the Kenley Players. Trained in musical theater, Stefani did everything from traveling and performing with a USO troupe to performing as the opening act for Barbara Mandrell, Chubby Checker, and the Oakridge Boys.

3

"I had an awesome childhood, but I decided that I didn't want to be a struggling musician my whole life," explains Stefani. "Besides, I had always been a news junkie. Working in broadcasting is what I really wanted to do."

Her dream of working in news came true when Channel 8 hired her right out of Mount Union College. Stefani remained at the station for 10 years, working as a reporter and anchor of the morning show until September of 2002, when she joined Channel 5 as one of the five o'clock news anchors.

It was during her career at Channel 8 that she and Roger connected.

"I was friends with someone who used to work at the station," explains Roger. "I called him and spoke with his wife to see if she knew if Stefani was dating anyone." His friend's wife wasn't sure but said she would call Stefani right away to find out.

"When she called me, she asked if I had happened to see some guy at La Dolce Vita, and she described Roger," remembers Stefani. "I didn't realize how well she knew Roger when I said, 'This guy is my destiny!' I went on and on and described him to a tee. She asked if she could give him my number. I said, 'No, don't! Let me have *his* number. I'm going to call him right now.' I did and we went out two days later."

Although there was an undeniable physical attraction between the two of them, it was during their first date that Stefani felt a deeper, more familiar feeling toward Roger.

"I always said that if I would ever meet a guy that was like my brother, I would marry him because my brother is just a good-natured, real sweet guy. That night I kept saying, 'Sorry I keep saying this, but you remind me so much of my brother.'"

The references that evening may have been brotherly, but the ambiance was anything but fraternal. Stefani's home at the time was a romantic, historic gatehouse on Lakeshore Boulevard. With her house as the setting, wine as the drink, and a sunset as the view, Stefani and Roger spent hours talking. By the second date, each of them knew: this was "the one."

"I was 35 at the time, never been married or engaged and had never really wanted to be," says Roger. "I knew by the second date that this was it for sure."

Stefani and Roger were so confident about their future together that two months later they traveled to California to visit Stefani's brother, and while there, they began to look at engagement rings. Although they shopped without the intention of buying, Roger kept the card from one of the stores and ordered a ring shortly after. That was in June. The proposal, however, didn't come until January. Roger held on to the ring not because he was unsure about popping the question, but because when he did pop the question, he wanted to do it in the most memorable way possible.

"I love to scuba dive," explains Roger. "Stefani had always been interested, but needed to become certified. I booked a trip to an incredible resort in St. Lucia, where Stefani took some tests and received certification."

Once the underwater technicalities were out of the way, Roger went to work to concoct a creative proposal that was undoubtedly romantic but full of possible glitches.

"On one of our dives, I brought three clamshells," explains Roger. "The first one was empty, the second one had a fake pearl inside of it, and the third one held the engagement ring. On the inside of the third clamshell I wrote, 'I love you. Marry me.'"

To insure that he could differentiate between the three clamshells, Roger had marked each one. So that the shells would not open, he had glued them shut and wrapped rubber bands around them. At the moment he wanted to propose to Stefani, he pulled all three shells out of his vest.

"I was underwater and very nervous," says Roger. "It was darker underwater, and all of a sudden I couldn't make out the pen lines on the shells. I pulled out one of the shells and realized the glue had worn away. I looked inside and it was empty. I threw it away thinking it was the empty one. I looked in the next shell and it was also empty."

At that point, Roger didn't know if the third shell was the one with the ring or if he had lost the ring. He opened the third shell and nearly dropped to the ocean floor in gratitude. The ring was still in the shell.

(As Roger is telling his proposal story, Stefani jumps up and reaches for a shadow box she has displayed on a table in their living room. Inside of the box are all three clamshells and a seahorse, imbedded in the sands of St. Lucia.)

"He called me over to him and pointed to a seahorse," says Stefani. "While I was looking at the seahorse, Roger pretended to scoop up a clamshell. He motioned to me to open it, but I didn't want to because I didn't want to disturb the clam. As soon as I looked closely at the clamshell, I saw the message and the ring. I started to cry."

For their wedding the following October, Stefani and Roger crossed the continent—and the ocean—to exchange their vows. "We didn't want a big wedding," explains Stefani. "We wanted it to be meaningful for us and not feel we were putting on a production for other people, so we invited our close friends and family to join us in Hawaii.

"My brother and mom gave me away on the beach with me wearing a simple but beautiful $48 dress and Roger wearing a tux with the pant legs rolled up. There was absolutely no stress. The day was about us and what our purpose was."

A year later, Stefani and Roger decided to try for children and now have two, a son and daughter. Although they feel blessed, it is in parenting that they find they are most different and occasionally disagree.

"We never had the slightest argument until we had kids and I'd find myself saying things like 'Roger, you're being too rough with him!'" says Stefani.

"In general, I tend to be laid back, admittedly, too laid back, and Stefani tends to be the worrier," says Roger. "If I might want to take our kids outside to build a snowman, Stefani might worry about it being too cold."

"When it comes to the kids, it's harder to compromise," explains Stefani, "because we both want to be the best parents we can be."

From scuba diving in the Red Sea off the coast of Egypt to bungee jumping off a bridge in Australia, Roger's adventuresome spirit is an integral part of who he is. Adventuresome to a point, Stefani admits she is much less of a risk-taker. They both realize, however, that their different approaches to adventure create a balance in their relationship that helps maintain harmony when it comes to parenting.

After five years of marriage, Stefani and Roger still have the same reaction to one another at the end of each day as they did the moment their eyes met at La Dolce Vita restaurant. Their hearts flutter.

"That instant connection is still there," asserts Stefani. "When we see each other at the end of the day, it still feels like we just started dating. Years ago, I remember thinking that someday I would want to be able to look at my husband after being married for a while and still be crazy for him. And you know what? I am!"

"I Can Dance with My Heart"

MARY LOU & JIM BEERS

As Mary Lou Beers talks about her marriage, her eyes remain steadfastly on her husband's face and her hand hovers close to his. She waits for a signal telling her that Jim wants to "spell" his thoughts and feelings.

Because two strokes have left Jim almost entirely paralyzed, he and Mary Lou have a unique way of communicating. Without the use of his legs, his arms, or his voice, Jim depends largely on the alphabet and Mary Lou to express himself.

"We've learned to talk to each other by going through the alphabet," says Mary Lou. "Jim squeezes my hand to let me know if the word he is spelling begins with a letter in the first or second half of the alphabet. Once I start listing the letters, he squeezes my hand to spell out what he wants to say, one letter at a time."

This sounds like a laborious and tedious way to communicate, but the Beerses make it seem effortless. After 30 years of "spelling," they are masters at listening not only with their eyes and ears, but also with their hearts.

As this couple joyously shares their dating days with me, Mary Lou leans over a basket filled with photographs and hands me their senior prom photo. I look up from the photograph to hear a computerized voice saying, "I am a fox." With pillows propped under the computer to hold it steady on his lap, Jim pushes a button to communicate preprogrammed phrases.

Mary Lou hands me more photos from their youth and describes the moment she met her husband. "I fell in love at 17 while getting on a school bus. When I first laid eyes on Jim, I saw his spirit. I watched how he related to others on the bus, and I knew I wanted to be a part of that."

Jim hits another button on his computer. "I am Mr. Nice Guy."

Ironically, before this couple got married, it was Mary Lou's life that was in jeopardy. After several dizzy spells and fainting episodes, Jim convinced her to have a heart catheterization, after which the doctors discovered that Mary Lou had a hole in her heart. She prepared herself to have what was a very serious operation back in the 1960s.

"I really thought I was going to die on the operating table," recalls Mary Lou. "I told Jim that if I died, I didn't want him going to a cemetery to grieve. Instead, I told him that every time he saw a red rose, I wanted him to give it a wink."

From that moment on, red roses became significant in their marriage, particularly after Jim's strokes.

Mary Lou remembers the day Jim had his first stroke. "I was seven months pregnant with our fourth child. He was driving on the freeway on his way home from work when all of a sudden he didn't feel very good. He pulled off to the side of the road and collapsed at the wheel. That was May of 1971. By July, although one arm was paralyzed, his speech was slurred, and he walked with a limp, he was back at work."

In July of 1973, doctors found another blocked carotid artery, and in September Jim underwent surgery twice. He made it through both operations, but had a stroke in post-op. After 3 months in intensive care, the doctors weaned Jim off the respirator and sent him to another hospital to recuperate for the next 10 months.

"When Jim finally came home from the hospital, he was six feet, three inches tall and weighed 83 pounds," remembers Mary

Lou. "Even though he couldn't eat, swallow, or sit up in a wheelchair, he was very alert. I knew from day one that he was conscious of everything."

As if this couple hadn't been through enough, the following years presented an even bigger obstacle—one that almost ended their marriage.

"I'll never forget it," says Mary Lou. "It was a couple of years after Jim's surgeries. I was busy raising four kids and trying to bring in some income by baking cakes in our home. Out of the blue, Jim spelled out that he wanted a divorce. I couldn't believe what he was saying. Here I had spent all of this time taking care of him and raising our children and he was telling me he wasn't happy.

"When I asked him why he wanted a divorce, he spelled, 'I want a wife.' When I asked him, 'What do you think I am?' he spelled, 'I could pay a nurse. I want a wife.'"

Mary Lou was distraught and angry that night, but she knew she had to hoist her husband onto her back and carry him upstairs to the bedroom as she had done for many months. She put Jim into bed and spent the next eight hours in the bathroom praying.

"I remember crying and praying all night long," says Mary Lou. "Even though Jim had said some things I didn't want to hear, I loved him. I just didn't know how to love him. At one point, I actually remember hearing God's voice say to me, 'He just wants a wife.' It was then that I realized I had never taken a vow to be a mother, a teacher, or a caregiver. But I had taken a vow to be a wife."

Dawn broke the following day, and Mary Lou walked out of the bathroom to start her morning routine. Once she had sent her four children off to school, she sat down with Jim and spelled. Their hands intertwined, frantically pressing and releasing, as Jim expressed his dreams for their marriage.

"I want to go out to dinner," spelled Jim. "I want to go to movies. I want to make love. I want to dance."

Mary Lou looked puzzled.

"I can dance with my heart," Jim assured her. "Just hold me. I want to be intimate with you."

Realizing there wasn't any reason why she couldn't do any of the things Jim was asking of her, she decided to take her husband on a date. With a blender in hand to liquefy his food, and a romantic mood in her heart, Mary Lou took Jim to a restaurant to enjoy an intimate, candlelit dinner.

"I knew people were staring at us at the restaurant, but I didn't care," says Mary Lou. "We had a great time sitting and rocking in each other's arms. When we got home that night, we attempted to make love. It was different, but I loved Jim so much."

From the one attempt at lovemaking came nothing short of a miracle. Mary Lou became pregnant.

"I could not believe it," remembers Mary Lou. "I was so scared. We had no hospitalization. I didn't know how we were going to do it, but when I gave Jim the news, he gave me a big thumbs up."

Jim's thumbs up turned out to be a providential gesture in more ways than one. After Mary Lou delivered their fifth child, a baby girl, the obstetrician was so touched by their love and faith that he canceled his bill.

By 1979, Jim was getting used to miracles in his life and wanted more of them. That is when he told Mary Lou he wanted to travel to Lourdes, France, for a healing. Although she wasn't sure how she was going to carry a paralyzed body onto a plane and travel for 20 hours, she agreed to take Jim overseas.

"I'll never forget walking into our hotel room in France," says Mary Lou. "There were 18 red roses waiting for us with a note that read, 'I believe in miracles. So should you.' The friend who had sent the roses had never known the significance of that particular flower."

The following day Jim and Mary Lou bathed at Lourdes. Without clothing, each of them was immersed into a concrete tub of water as both hoped and prayed for a healing. When Mary Lou saw Jim after her immersion, she found him with eyes dancing and a thumb shooting straight up to the sky.

Jim spelled to Mary Lou, "I had my miracle! In the water, I realized that it doesn't matter if you can't walk and talk. All that matters is that you can love, and I can love."

In light of the fact that they each felt they had given birth to a new life while in Lourdes, Jim and Mary Lou decided to renew their vows before going home. With the world's most ill as their witnesses—the blind, the deaf, and the crippled—Mary Lou and Jim exchanged new wedding rings and new vows.

"I remember getting ready to board the plane to go home," says Mary Lou. "It had been raining. Before entering the plane, I looked up and saw the biggest rainbow. A woman traveling with us said that was our sign that we'd be back. We've been back 10 times since and have brought friends with us each time."

Their trips to Lourdes solidified their already strong faith and helped prepare them for more startling news that they received two years ago. Jim's legs had to be amputated.

"Gangrene had set in, in the left leg first," remembers Mary Lou. "The doctor told Jim that he had the right to die, but Jim looked at him and said, 'Cut them off. I want to love my wife awhile longer.'"

It was when Jim had the right leg amputated a year later that life changed the most dramatically.

"His right leg was the one he'd always use to wake me up or wrap around me to give me a hug," explains Mary Lou. "His right leg was his lifeline."

During the second amputation, Jim was told he would have to remain awake during the surgery because his heart wasn't strong enough to withstand general anesthesia. Although under the influence of a spinal, Jim was conscious of everyone and everything in the operating room.

Because he was to be awake during the surgery, Jim had requested a friend be by his side in the operating room. Just as the surgeons were about to remove his right leg, Jim spelled to his friend to tell the doctors to wait. They did and Jim spelled, "I'm letting go of this rotten ship so I can sail free."

Although Jim has lost his legs, he has gained a peace that eludes many. Both he and Mary Lou recognize that the love between a husband and wife need not depend on an arm to hug with, a leg to wrap with, or a voice to speak with. The human spirit can transcend the body, and when that happens, love sails free.

Hard at Play

ERIC & ROBIN BENZLÉ

Cross the threshold of the Benzlé home and you enter a world of imagination, creativity, and plain old-fashioned fun. As you walk from room to room, you can't help but inhale this couple's love of travel and entertaining.

"We wanted each room in our house to have a distinct personality," says Robin. "We have a Roman bathroom inspired by going to Italy and an African bathroom because we love African art."

"Seventy-five percent of the things in our house are related to travel or our fascination with a particular culture," explains Eric.

Robin's flair for the dramatic when it comes to living spaces can be traced back to her grandfather, Monroe Copper, Jr., and her father, Monroe Copper III. Both renowned Cleveland architects, they designed a large number of homes in Gates Mills and Shaker Heights.

As a designer and builder who started his own business from scratch, Eric has an eye for detail that comes from having an artistic mother. His can-do attitude stems from being raised by parents who gave him the green light whenever he wanted to replace walls in a bathroom or finish a basement.

"What my parents did for me was great," says Eric, "but looking back on it, I'm not sure I would have entrusted my house to a high school kid. Because of my parents' support, I was able to gain experience over the years by reading and doing."

Robin professes to be as self-taught as her husband, but her entrepreneurial bent started with cooking rather than construction. Inventing recipes has always felt natural to her.

"I've been cooking my entire life, and it all started with a Hasbro Easy-Bake oven," says Robin. "I used to pack lunches for my father before he'd go off to work. I'd mix up awful things for him like oatmeal, tuna, and raisins."

As an adult, Robin's passion for cooking led her to write and self-publish a book called *Cooking with Humor* in 1991 and in 1993 to co-write a cookbook with Tom Wilson, the creator of *Ziggy*. While promoting her books, she became a weekly radio talk-show guest on the Lee Kirk Show on WWWE AM. During that time she met Trapper Jack, the morning host on Light Rock 106.5 FM, the sister station to WWWE.

"Whenever I would go in to do the show with Lee Kirk, I'd always see Trapper, and we'd really hit it off," says Robin. "He was quick on his feet, and I could keep up with him. When he got a job with WDOK 102.1 FM, he called me and asked if I'd want to cohost the morning show with him. That was eight years ago, and I've been doing the show ever since."

Before they became entrepreneurs, there was a time when Robin and Eric worked in a more traditional setting as employees of a computer sales company. It was there that they met.

"I remember talking to Eric at a going-away party for a coworker," says Robin. "When Eric was hired, I had confused him with another job applicant who had lived in Florida and was married with kids. It wasn't until I asked him how his kids liked Cleveland winters that he told me he wasn't married."

While Robin was confused about Eric's identity, Eric was confused about Robin's age.

"We worked across the hall from each other," recalls Eric. "One day I heard Robin telling one of her customers that she was 38 years old. Being 25 at the time, I figured there was too much of an age difference between us. It wasn't until we talked at the going-away party that I learned she had been joking with her customer. She was really 28."

That night after the party, Eric walked Robin out to her car. Silence hung in the air until Robin broke it by saying, "Well, don't just stand there. Ask me out!"

Their first date was an afternoon at Robin's place followed by a home-cooked dinner. Extremely confident about her cooking skills, she planned what she was sure would be an impressive meal.

"It was the worst meal I had ever prepared," says Robin. "I overcooked the pork chops to the point that when Eric tried to cut them, the table shook so badly the wine spilled out of the glasses. I overcooked the cauliflower so much that I had to try to pass it off as mashed potatoes."

Robin's dinner may have been overdone, but that didn't put the brakes on the freight-train momentum of their relationship. Two weeks later, Eric took Robin to Hilton Head to meet his parents, but more importantly, to propose.

"My response, a famous story for people who know us," says Robin, "was 'What took you so long?'"

Twenty-five years and two daughters later, Robin and Eric credit a lot of their marital longevity to play rather than work.

"You know, you always hear that you really have to work at a marriage," says Robin. "We don't work at our marriage. We play at it."

"Not everyone is the same," says Eric. "Some people don't know how to have fun, and that's a problem."

Not for this couple. And their imagination goes beyond creating distinctly different rooms in their home—occasionally they will even assume the roles of movie characters and act like those characters for 24 hours.

"We like to get into creative playacting," says Eric. "We just take a subject or character and run with it to be silly."

Both Robin and Eric appreciate slapstick humor and have been known to make friends laugh by being funny in a physical way.

Robin recalls a dinner party they hosted where Eric left the table and returned looking rather odd.

"I remember Eric coming back to the table looking awfully beefy," says Robin. "He glanced around at everyone and said, 'You know, it's terribly warm in here. I think I'm going to take off my shirt.' When he took off his shirt, there was another shirt underneath. When he took off that shirt, there was another shirt underneath that one. Nineteen shirts later, everyone was howling with laughter."

As silly and fun-loving as Eric can be at times, he is dead serious when it comes to a particular aspect of his marriage.

"It's a quirky thing, but it's always been something I believe in," says Eric. "We don't ever mention the word divorce in a context that relates to either one of us or our marriage. It isn't something that is even a remote consideration, and, therefore, it's one word that doesn't get mentioned."

Robin becomes philosophical when she talks about her marriage to Eric.

"I feel like I am lucky enough to live with the finest gentleman I've ever met in my life. On top of that, he's the funniest person I've ever hung around with. I understand that what we have is an unusual thing. I appreciate the fact that this is not a normal marriage. It's a little luck, a little fate, and a whole lot of chemistry."

On any given day, if you were to visit the Benzlé home, you might catch Robin and Eric sitting at the "Benzlé Bar." Custom designed and built into the corner of the living room, it is a favorite spot in their house.

"One of the most romantic things I can think of is the two of us sitting at the Benzlé Bar and just talking," says Eric. "I have more fun doing that than anything else."

Well, almost anything. Avid Scrabble players, this couple devotes a good chunk of time each week to word play. Careful to hold on to their "s" tiles or save a high-scoring letter for a triple word square, Eric and Robin take playing the game seriously. Anyone who knows them knows they not only work hard, they play hard.

Wait for the Nectar

KRSNANANDINI DEVI DASI
& TARIQ SALEEM ZIYAD

"On paper, we have every reason for getting divorced," says Tariq.

His wife, Krsnanandini, chuckles and nods her head in agreement. "God must have a really good sense of humor."

Married 13 years—a second marriage for both of them—this couple started life together with extraordinary challenges. Blending two families from previous marriages is not an unusual scenario upon beginning a second marriage. Blending two families to create one with 16 children, however, *is* unusual, especially when you have 3 more children together, bringing the tally up to a grand total of 19.

And this couple has had not only to raise a large family, but to do so in a household where two very different religions are practiced. Tariq is Muslim, and Krsnanandini is a devotee of the Hare Krishna movement.

"People couldn't understand how with two such different religions, we would be able to make our relationship work," says Tariq.

"It really doesn't matter that in the Islamic religion there are no images of God, for example, but that in the Hare Krishna religion, divine personalities are depicted in scriptures," asserts

Krsnanandini. "What matters is that we both worship the same God."

Their dedication to living a spiritual life is the axis around which their marriage turns.

"It is so important to have some spiritual principle you subscribe to in your marriage," says Krsnanandini. "Because when the storm comes, and storms are going to come, you need to be committed to more than physical and material needs."

Tariq agrees. "If couples have a sense that there's a spiritual value in all that they are struggling to do, and if they are patient, have faith, and wait for the nectar, the nectar will come."

The nectar that Tariq speaks of is a state of grace in which two people build a life together based on trust, respect, and the knowledge that there is a divine purpose to their lives and their marriage.

The state of grace that Tariq and Krsnanandini so often find themselves in was not always present in their marriage, however. During their first two years of matrimony, this couple came very close to separating. In fact, Krsnanandini went so far as to pack up Tariq's belongings and put them in his mother's backyard.

"Tariq had a lot of issues from his past relationship that haunted us," remembers Krsnanandini. "We tried to work through the issues, but couldn't do it alone."

In a final effort to make the marriage work, Krsnanandini contacted a friend who was a minister and asked him to meet with both of them. Unbeknownst to her, Tariq had made the exact same phone call to the exact same friend, a coincidence they now look upon as divine intervention.

"I remember driving to the meeting," says Krsnanandini. "I was crying and praying, 'Lord, I think you're asking too much of me.' Suddenly, I felt a sense of deep peace and I heard a voice say to me, 'You can go ahead and leave Tariq and it will be justified, but better than that would be to work with your husband.' I knew then that Tariq needed me and that we were going to work out our problems."

"Don't think that just because negative things happen in your marriage that that's enough to give up," says Tariq. "You've got to wait and keep stirring the pot until you get the nectar. It takes faith and trust. Even if you're not real good at being a spiritual person, if you keep trying, you're going to get to that sweet stuff."

On top of their commitment to their own marriage, Tariq and Krsnanandini are also on a mission to help other couples drink this marital mead. This couple, both of whom have degrees in psychology, education, and business, founded the Dasi-Ziyad Family Institute in 1997 in Cleveland. They dedicated this organization to the utilization of spiritual principles, techniques, and skills to support the healthy development of marriage, family, and community.

Whether they are conducting marriage-enrichment workshops, writing a curriculum for a school youth project, or counseling couples in their home, Tariq and Krsnanandini recognize that their marriage is part of a divine arrangement designed to help keep communities and families healthy.

The inspiration to do the work they do as a couple came to Krsnanandini at an early age. "I was 19 when I was initiated into the Hare Krishna movement," explains Krsnanandini. "My spiritual teacher, my swami, inspired me for the rest of my life. After he passed away in 1977, I had a dream in which he gave me an instruction to show people how to have God-conscious marriages. Because of the respect I had for my spiritual teacher, I would never have questioned his guidance, even though I wasn't even married at the time."

Krsnanandini held on to that dream and waited for the right time and for the right person to help realize her vision. The right time was 12 years later. The right person was Tariq.

Although they first met when Krsnanandini was 8 years old and Tariq was 19, they didn't reconnect until Krsnanandini was an adult.

"I was actually reintroduced to Tariq by my ex-husband," says Krsnanandini. "Tariq's father had been a mentor to him."

Years later, after her divorce, Krsnanandini read a book that mentioned how important it was for single mothers to find someone they respected to mentor their sons. Krsnanandini had spent enough time with Tariq to know that he was the one she wanted as a mentor for her boys.

"Up until that point, we were just seeing each other occasionally," recalls Tariq. "But when Krsnanandini asked me to be a mentor to her sons, I knew that meant I would be seeing her more often."

Shortly after that, Tariq invited Krsnanandini to a Christmas party, which she went to even though, at the time, she rarely socialized because of her busy school schedule. Attending a social gathering together led them to perceive each other in a different light, and consider their relationship as potentially more than purely platonic.

After the party, Tariq and Krsnanandini started seeing more of each other. One of their outings was a trip to Detroit to see an inspirational speaker. While there, Krsnanandini stayed with her brother, who put her through an exercise that changed her life.

"My brother and I sat up all night talking," recalls Krsnanandini. "He asked me to make a list of qualities that I would want in a husband. I made that list and we prayed over it. As I looked over the list of qualities, I realized that Tariq had every one of them."

Although Tariq was quick to come up with reasons not to commit himself to Krsnanandini, one fact was undeniable. They were kindred spirits. Their devotion to their own spirituality and to encouraging spirituality in others has made them realize they were meant to be a couple.

Different Ways to Make God Laugh

Noah & Sharon Budin

"It was a test. I slowly lowered my hand down the pole until it just touched hers. When she didn't move her hand away from mine, I knew I had a shot," says Noah, recalling the night he and Sharon first rode the El in Chicago.

That evening Sharon and some friends had gone into the city to hear Noah sing. He was in a group that had become a popular Chicago entertainment phenomenon called "Four Guys Standing Around Singing."

"We used to sing in the park at Chicago's Water Tower," says Noah, "and would usually attract several hundred people who liked to listen to doo-wop harmony. We weren't licensed, but because the police liked us, they looked the other way."

The night Sharon watched Noah perform, she witnessed her future husband come very close to being arrested. A newspaper reporter for the *Chicago Sun-Times* had written a review of the group, giving them prime exposure and giving the police a reason to lower the boom.

"All we did was stand on the steps and sing one note when the police came running over, shined their lights on us, and announced through their megaphones that we had to clear the area," remembers Noah. "That was our first date."

"Six weeks later, we were engaged," says Sharon.

Later that year, at Thanksgiving, Noah and Sharon drove to Cleveland to announce their engagement. It was then they realized their different religious backgrounds might cause some family discord. Noah is Jewish, and although he had not been raised in a strict religious environment, his family still maintained some Jewish traditions. Sharon, who was a seminary student at the time, had been raised in a devout Christian home with a father who was a Presbyterian minister.

"I remember the day I met Noah's family I was so nervous I was nauseated," says Sharon.

"When Sharon met my parents, we sensed there was so much of a problem with her not being Jewish that we postponed announcing the engagement to my family until after we told Sharon's parents," admits Noah.

Sharon's parents, who Noah and Sharon had thought would object to their engagement, were not only thrilled about the idea, they suggested that her father officiate at the wedding. Once Sharon and Noah got back to Chicago, they called his parents and announced their wedding plans. Although their initial reaction was lukewarm, they soon warmed up to the idea and fell in love with Sharon. Within weeks Noah's mother and father visited Sharon's parents in Detroit.

"Our mothers hit it off," remembers Sharon. "Our dads, well . . . Noah's dad was a hardened Democrat, and my dad is a staunch Republican. Because the women were all for us getting married, the men had no choice but to follow along."

Once their families got to know each other and accepted the fact that their children were going to be married regardless of their different religious upbringings, they set out to transform Noah and Sharon's idea of a small wedding into a wedding reception with 350 guests and 1,000 blintzes, made by Noah's mother.

"Five years later, I was still pulling blintzes out of the freezer," says Sharon.

"We looked for a rabbi to co-officiate the service, but realized we weren't going to find anyone to do an interfaith wedding," remembers Noah. "In our research, we found that according to Jewish tradition, it wasn't necessary to have a rabbi marry us in order to be spiritually wed. We figured since Sharon's father was the minister and [his officiation was] legally binding according to the state, it would be cool if my father would do the Jewish part of the service. They collaborated and wrote the ceremony together. So, we were married by our fathers: a Christian Republican and a Jewish Democrat."

Married 17 years, Noah and Sharon have passed down religious diversity to their three children. When their oldest son was three years old, Sharon and Noah talked with him about the differences between Christians and Jews, and between going to church and going to temple. When Sharon asked their son if he understood what they were trying to tell him, he responded by saying, "Sure Mom, there's one God and we all have different ways to make him laugh."

"What our son said is so true," says Sharon, now studying to be a Presbyterian minister herself. "Even though we work in different religious settings, Noah and I have more in common about our faith and our relationship with God than we have differences."

"I've learned so much more about my own religion because of being with Sharon, and I am equally comfortable sitting in a church as I am worshiping in a synagogue," says Noah.

Sharon and Noah have gone against conventional wisdom when it comes to raising their children in an interfaith family. They had heard that it is best to choose one faith and raise the children in that faith so that they are not confused, or put in the position of having to choose one parent's religion over the other's.

"We believe our kids are smarter than that," says Sharon. "They are going to make their own choice along the way anyway. If they choose a temple, that's fine. If they choose a church, that's fine. We just want to give them as much of an opportunity to live in the love of God as possible."

"Everybody has a choice," says Noah. "As long as our children are part of a faith community, that's what is most important to us."

Although Noah and Sharon agree completely on how to raise their children in an interfaith marriage, they are not always on the same page when it comes to other issues. As an entertainer, singer, and songwriter, Noah is grateful for Sharon's steady, predictable salary. Sharon, however, sometimes feels financial pressure from that responsibility.

"I'm not a pragmatist by nature," explains Sharon. "I'm that way because one of us has to be. There are times when it puts stress on our marriage."

"We're learning how to manage that stress, but it takes work," says Noah. "We've had some marriage counseling along the way. I think if people need help, they should go to counseling. You can't do anything in this world in a vacuum. You need support."

Noah describes their marriage as having peaks and valleys. At the peaks, Noah is often making Sharon laugh.

"One of the things I love most about Sharon is that she laughs at me," says Noah. "It's like that old joke about the actor who says, 'Well enough about me. Let's talk about you. What have *you* seen me in?'"

After Noah waits for Sharon to stop laughing, he goes on to say he also loves the fact that his wife has a balance of creativity and practicality. He explains that she can be artistic but has a work ethic that is different from his.

"He's the balloon and I'm the string," says Sharon.

Not quite sure if he likes that analogy, Noah imitates the voice of a commentator at a parade and says, "Here comes Noah, floating down the street."

"Well, maybe not a Macy's Thanksgiving Day Parade balloon," responds Sharon. "More like a birthday-party balloon."

They both laugh and realize that Sharon truly is the grounding force to Noah's free-floating spirit.

You Are One Person's World

MARTHA & DEL DONAHOO

Upon entering the home of the Donahoos, I knew I was in a place where memories had not only been made, but memorialized. Photographs of places they'd been, sketches of loved ones, including their beloved cat, Cookie, and trinkets from days gone by fill each room of their lakefront home in Bay Village.

Windowsills lined with baubles and souvenirs create a backdrop for the one thing in their home that speaks the loudest about their love: a shiny black baby grand piano. This musical instrument is a symbol and daily reminder to Martha of how dearly loved she is by Del.

"I'll never forget it," says Martha. "I had just had a heart catheterization, and the doctors told me my heart was fine. Del was so grateful I was okay that he leaned over me with tears in his eyes and whispered, 'You're getting a baby grand piano.'"

Music has always been a big part of Martha's life and was what eventually led to her meeting her husband. As the pianist at her cousin's wedding, she was able to get a bird's-eye view of Del, who was the best man at the wedding and a guy she thought had an incredible voice.

"I remember I was standing at the reception, and Martha walked by me and pinched my little finger," says Del. "I thought, *At least she knows I'm alive.*"

Their first meeting led to their first date at Drake University's homecoming game in Des Moines, Iowa, Martha's hometown. Dressed in green with a beanie atop her red hair, Martha won Del's heart. Shortly after came a proposal and a marriage that has lasted 55 years.

When asked to what they attribute their nuptial longevity, Del and Martha talk about teamwork.

"I grew up during the Depression," explains Martha. "My father lost all of his money in 1931 and had to start all over again. My mom and dad put their heads together and created their own business, which they ran from our home. My sister ran the office, and when my older brother came home from junior high school and I came home from grade school, we did office work. We learned that we had to work together."

Growing up in a farming town in Iowa, Del had an upbringing similar to Martha's in that working as a team was a family value. With wood to be chopped and land to be farmed, his family often ate at nine o'clock in the evening and woke up at five o'clock in the morning to make sure that what had to get done got done.

That sense of responsibility has transferred over to the Donahoo marriage.

"We've come to depend upon each other," says Del. "There's a feeling of responsibility to each other. I know I can count on Martha to do what needs to be done for the good of the union."

Early in their marriage, Del's career dictated that he move from Iowa to Omaha, then to Kansas City, and finally to Cleveland in 1968 to take a job as an anchor and general-assignment reporter. He feels blessed not only to have never been without a job, but also to have had a wife who would follow him wherever the job would take him.

Today, when Del has to leave the house early to follow the often unpredictable schedule of a television broadcaster, he knows he can depend on Martha to be there for him even if it means getting up at three o'clock in the morning.

"It's a lot easier to come downstairs with the lights on, coffee brewing, and someone you love waiting for you in the kitchen than to stumble around alone in the dark," says Del. "I've never asked her to do this. I've never told her to do this. She's just always done it."

As far as conflict in their marriage is concerned, Del and Martha say they've never disagreed on how to raise their two children, Marcelaine and Dennis, how to handle the finances, or how to have sex, which Del is quick to add does not end at age 50.

"We've never disagreed on anything that was important," insists Del.

"That's not to say we don't irritate each other," adds Martha.

"Oh, no," agrees Del. "We're real good at doing that."

Irritations aside, this couple credits their mostly harmonious relationship to two things: the ability to discuss disagreements sooner than later and their strong connection to their church.

"Spirituality in a marriage is important," asserts Del. "Sometimes it's puzzling, but neither of us has doubted the spiritual aspect of ourselves or of our union."

Martha agrees. "We don't analyze our faith. It's just a natural part of ourselves."

After more than half a century of marriage, both Del and Martha feel grateful for what they've had together. They view their partnership as an example of lifelong teamwork, a venue for their own spiritual growth and that of their family, and a true blessing.

"I want to tell you about a quote I read recently in the newspaper," says Del. "It describes what Martha and I have together. 'To the world you are just one person, but in some cases, you are one person's world.'" Martha couldn't agree more.

No Other Bridge to Cross

KELLEY & DAVID WORDEN

It is widely known. Losing a child puts a couple at higher-than-average risk for divorce. After 21 years of marriage, Kelley and David Worden are that couple. Regardless, they successfully fight the odds that are so heavily stacked against them.

When Kelley and David sent their 15-year-old son Jason to Myrtle Beach with Kelley's sister and parents and Jason's older brother Dave, they felt confident that the family would enjoy their vacation.

"My parents owned a time-share condo in Myrtle Beach, a place where we had vacationed with the kids since they were little," explains Kelley. "Although I had just had surgery and couldn't make the trip, our kids, Jason in particular, wanted to go. When he brought his progress report home and we saw his grades were acceptable, we said he could travel along."

On May 12, 2000, Jason, his older brother, his aunt, and his grandparents drove to Myrtle Beach. While traveling southbound on Route 77 near the border of West Virginia and Virginia, they encountered a pickup truck that had lost some pieces of furniture on the northbound side of Route 77. The truck suddenly turned off onto the median to retrieve the furniture. As they tried to avoid hitting the swerving car ahead of them, the car Jason and his aunt were in was propelled across the highway, rolling over twice, and Jason was thrown from the vehicle.

"Jason wore his seat belt religiously," says Kelley. "My sister noticed that he had the belt on during the entire trip, but for some reason the last time he got into the car, he must not have buckled up. My sister thinks he had put his headphones on and had fallen asleep."

That evening David and Kelley received a call every parent fears, a call telling them their son had been in an accident.

"When I phoned the emergency room of the hospital Jason had been life-flighted to and talked to the doctor, he told me Jason had been thrown from the car and had suffered a massive head injury. When he explained there had been gray matter at the scene, I knew he was brain dead."

Kelley and David boarded the first plane out of Cleveland to Charleston, West Virginia. When they arrived at the hospital, they found their son in the intensive care unit, attached to life support.

"After the staff did several EEGs, there was no brain function," remembers Kelley. "David and I knew Jason well enough to know he wouldn't have wanted to live like that. The one positive thing we could get from removing Jason from life support was that we decided to donate his organs."

David and Kelley agree that one reason their marriage has survived the loss of their son is because of the support they received from many of their friends and the kids who attended Jason's wake.

"There was such an outpouring of love from students," remembers David. "The wake was packed with kids who lifted us up."

"At the funeral, we asked people to write memories of Jason," says Kelley. "One of the things we kept hearing was that Jason always went out of his way to make people who were on the fringe feel included. One story that meant a lot to us was about a girl in Jason's gym class who apparently was not athletic, and a little overweight. After Jason died, she went to her counselor and said,

'I didn't know this boy very well, but he was in my gym class. Whenever anyone else was captain of the team, they would pick me last. When Jason was captain, he made me feel special because he always picked me first.'"

To help kids remember Jason and to carry on his legacy of character, Kelley and David began a youth mentoring club called J.A.Y.S. Club, the letters of which stand for Jesus At Your Side. The primary mission of the club is to equip kids with the tools to build good character, honesty, integrity, fairness, and caring so as to prepare them for leadership roles as adults. To help people learn more about the club, a website is available at www.jaysclub.org.

Realizing they needed professional help to get through the tragedy of losing a child, Kelley and David went to a support group called Compassionate Friends.

"While we were going to counseling and to Compassionate Friends, I remember feeling as if Dave wasn't grieving," says Kelley. "What I learned was that each of us had our own way of grieving. At one of the meetings, David said something really profound. He said, 'I miss Jason, but I know that our children don't belong to us. They're just lent to us. If we really want the best for our children, and we believe in heaven and God, then it's rather selfish for us to want them back.'"

"Of course we hurt and of course the loss is there," says David, "but we grieve because we're so used to having them with us. I know that one day I will see Jason again. Now I have something to look forward to during my last days on earth."

When Kelley and David look back on the loss of their son, they realize that if it hadn't been for the marriage counseling they had had a year before, their relationship may not have survived.

A few years before their son's death, David began feeling an uncontrollable desire for change in his life.

"I was 44 years old and constantly thinking about whether I was happy as a person and in my marriage," remembers David. "At the time, I had been at a job for 19 years, and I was frustrated.

"I had always been the kind of person who hadn't done a lot of different things in life. I got to a point where I wanted to go out and do something I'd never done before. Guys at work would always go out afterwards for a drink, but I was an eight-to-five guy who went home for dinner every night."

In David's quest to find himself as an individual, he became emotionally involved with a female coworker who was going through a similar situation. Feeling a connection to one another, they began having lunch together and drinks after work.

"The night I celebrated my 10th anniversary as a nurse at the hospital I had been working at, David didn't come home in time to go with me to the celebration," says Kelley. "When I came home later that night, he told me that he didn't think he wanted to be married anymore. Looking back on it, even though I was in shock, I knew we had been leading separate lives for a long time."

After the shock waves settled, Kelley realized she hadn't gotten married to get divorced and told David she wanted the two of them to see a marriage counselor.

"I give David a lot of credit," says Kelley. "He not only went through sessions with me, he went to counseling for his own issues."

After a year of therapy, the counselor felt David and Kelley weren't progressing, so it was suggested that they participate in a therapeutic separation. During that time, they were not to date anyone else, continue to have family time with their children, and plan dates for the two of them.

While David lived with his sister, Kelley worked two jobs and raised the children. It was a desperate time for her.

"I remember feeling like a failure," says Kelley. "My doctor had me on some medication, and I seriously thought about taking the bottle of pills. I went to our marriage counselor's office at one o'-clock in the morning so that I could speak with her, but security was called to escort me to an emergency room. It was after that experience that David and I looked at each other and said, 'What are we both doing?'"

With the help of counseling, Kelley recognized that David's attraction to another woman had much to do with the fact that he felt needed and appreciated by her.

"That was one thing I had to take ownership of," says Kelley. "I hadn't given David the honor and respect over the years that he deserved. David owned the fact that he needed to put effort and attention into his marriage rather than an outside relationship."

Therapy, along with information they acquired from some relationship experts, inspired this Brook Park couple to begin courting each other again.

"As soon as we started dating, I began to feel butterflies, after 15 years of marriage," admits Kelley. "We started to do things like we used to do. One time I surprised David and kidnapped him from work. Another time, he made me breakfast in bed."

David and Kelley agree that if they had not gone through such a difficult time in their relationship and had not grown stronger for having gone through it, their marriage would most likely not have survived the loss of their son.

"After we lost Jason, I had to get my priorities straight," says David. "I had to ask myself what was important, me busting my rear for the company I worked for or pursuing what I really wanted to do. I decided to go back to school and become certified as a Microsoft Certified Systems Engineer."

When Kelley and David talk about what has kept them together, they point to their faith.

"Kelley has always been involved in our church, whereas I had never really been actively involved. I was shy and felt it wasn't time. Suddenly, after we lost Jason, it was time. I began to give back to the church through music by bringing my guitar to service and singing. I'm now the contemporary service coordinator and chairman of the music committee. My relationship with the Lord has kept me on track with who I am as an individual, as a spouse, and as a dad."

David feels his relationship with God is not only his ticket to a happy marriage, but also a ticket to eventually seeing his son.

"There is no other bridge for me to cross in order to see Jason except for the one that God is at the center of. That's how I will meet my son again."

She Says Tom(ay)to,
He Says Tom(ah)to

LINDA & FRED GRIFFITH

For someone who has been a television personality for decades, broadcasting news, sharing recipes, and interviewing thousands of prominent people, you'd never guess he would be as shy as he is. But it is his quiet, unassuming demeanor that drew Linda to Fred Griffith.

"I was attracted to Fred's gentleness and quietness," says Linda. "He broadened my taste in music tremendously. He even got me interested in camping. I'm Jewish. I don't camp."

That he thought Linda was terrific for her proactive personality certainly didn't diminish his appeal in her eyes. As director of the Cuyahoga County Hospital Foundation during the late 1970s, Linda was a mover and shaker who spearheaded benefits to raise money while working at Metro General Hospital.

"I was attracted to her being an activist," remembers Fred. "She was always pushing the envelope, always trying to make things happen, always organizing. I was impressed with what an efficient, strong, and bright person she was."

Fred and Linda agree that the difference in their personalities is what makes their marriage work so well. Whether they are traveling, cooking, or writing another book together, their opposite

43

approaches to situations bring balance and solidarity to their relationship.

"Linda is 180 degrees opposite from me in that I don't push to make things happen the way she does. I'm just a go-with-the-flow, okay-whatever-happens-is-fine-with-me kind of guy."

Fred's easygoing nature carries over to his approach to writing whenever he coauthors a cookbook with Linda—and at times chafes against her organized, plan-ahead style.

"Linda organizes the recipes way in advance, and I do my writing at the last minute," admits Fred. "I gather as much research as possible up until I have to begin writing the essays."

Although both agree that writing a book together is one of the most challenging projects a couple can tackle, they seem to have the secret formula for success, as evidenced by their sixth book, *Nuts* (St. Martin's Press, 2003).

For all the ways they are opposite, Fred and Linda are also similar, and in areas where they think it matters most.

"Our values are congruent," says Fred. "We appreciate the same things in society and in people. We both are positive in that we want to make the world better."

Fred's and Linda's interests are as vital to them as their values. Whether they are enjoying a symphony at Severance Hall or an exotic trip to the highlands of Papua New Guinea, or backpacking in the Adirondacks, they revel in their mutual appetite for adventure.

When asked to describe their most romantic memory, they couldn't agree. There were simply too many choices. Was it time spent swimming in the hot springs in China? Or the spontaneous drive through the French countryside? When Linda assured him it was their first couple of camping trips that made them feel the sharp point of Cupid's arrow, Fred didn't argue.

"Those first camping trips were quite wonderful," recalls Linda. "The weekend after we were married, we went off to the woods."

"We'd be in the woods for five, sometimes seven days and not see another soul," says Fred.

Although Linda and Fred enjoy leaving the city on adventuresome travels, their commitment to Cleveland has created ties that bind and aren't likely to unravel. Fred's ties to the city strengthened when he became news director at WEWS Channel 5 in 1967. So committed to Cleveland was he that when the opportunity arose to be on the staff of CBS News in New York doing radio, something he had done for WDOK in Cleveland, he declined the offer.

"After I started to do well in Cleveland, I had many opportunities to leave," remembers Fred, "but I stayed here because I liked the traditions here. I liked the fact that there had been strong support from the establishment people of the region, the industrialists, basically. They had put their money into the Cleveland Orchestra, the Museum of Art, and the Cleveland Play House. This town also had a tradition of good governance and concern for the citizens. That was why Cleveland was my city of choice when I was looking for a job in 1959."

And the relationship between Fred Griffith and Cleveland has been a reciprocal one. There is no doubt he took advantage of the wealth of opportunities this city offered him, but with every benefit he received, he made a matching gift. Over the years, he has been a member of a variety of councils and boards ranging from the Appalachian Action Council to the Rockefeller Brothers Study on Human Sexuality.

Linda is committed to Cleveland as well. "This city is a good place in which to live and raise a family and visit other places from. There is a sense of community here that is most unusual."

Although their love of Cleveland is one subject upon which they agree, Linda and Fred are not always of like mind when it comes to managing their relationships with others. Both have children from previous marriages, and they find that blending two families has been one of the biggest challenges in their marriage—a challenge that has caused them to become stronger as a couple.

"Surmounting major differences of opinion on managing our relationships with other people has been a challenge for us," admits Fred. "Linda is a more focused person than I and wants resolution and answers to problems. I tend to want to say that whatever the problem is, it doesn't matter and that everything will be okay. So I would say the issues we've had are basically a reflection of that difference in our personalities."

Undeniably, Linda and Fred are different people, as the license plates on each of their cars indicate. Linda's reads "onions" and Fred's reads "garlic." Add one or the other to a recipe, and the flavor becomes interesting. Combine them and the taste is heavenly.

Every Step Together

TENSIE & CLAUDE HOLLAND

They were both 18 years old, both graduates of the Cleveland Public Schools, both tall, both athletic, and both attending the University of Cincinnati, but what made Tensie and Claude feel like kindred spirits as much as campus sweethearts was the fact that each had lost a parent at a very young age.

Tensie was 8 years old and an only child when her mother died from breast cancer. Claude was 15 years old when his father passed away, after five years of living with multiple sclerosis.

Although Tensie and Claude's first meeting on campus was brief, it didn't take Claude long to realize he wanted to know more about the tall, slender, attractive girl he had encountered on the way to class. So, he called her. Four hours later, their conversation ended, as did the long-distance relationship between Claude and his girlfriend at another school.

"It was nice to be on campus and have someone in my life who was from my hometown," says Claude. "Tensie and I had a lot in common. She liked sports, and because I was a varsity athlete on campus, she would always attend my track meets and, on occasion, my practices.

"Where we found the most common ground was in the fact that we had both lost a parent. There is a void that occurs when

49

you lose a parent at such a young age. We learned how to fill that void for each other."

"Though the circumstances under which our parents died were completely different, we knew, even at a subconscious level, that losing a parent when we were so young created a special bond between us," says Tensie.

Once Claude and Tensie began dating in 1974, neither dated another person again. Whether they were seen on campus together at sorority or fraternity parties, sporting events, or the local sandwich shop, they were always thought of as an inseparable couple.

Tensie remembers the impression they made as a pair on campus. "All of our friends got used to the fact that where there was Claude, there was Tensie and where there was Tensie, there was Claude."

After graduating from college and entering their professions, Claude as a middle school history and music teacher and Tensie as a job classification counselor for the Cuyahoga County Probation Department, they were ready for what felt like the natural next step in their relationship.

"When you spend the kind of time with each other as we had spent, we knew there was only one other level to take it to, and that was marriage," says Claude. "It was pretty obvious that we were headed in that direction."

After an eight-year courtship, Claude asked Tensie's father for permission to marry her, and in August of 1982, they were wed. Now married 21 years, this Cleveland couple has a theory as to why their relationship has been successful.

"We have experienced so many things for the first time together that it has helped solidify and cement our marriage," says Claude.

"We applied for our first jobs together, bought our first cars together, and later in life we lost our jobs at the same time," explains Tensie. "We've grown up together through our twenties, thirties, and forties."

At the age of 32, Tensie suffered three losses: her job, her father, and her breast. During that time, the solid foundation Claude and Tensie had laid for their marriage paid off in a big way.

"My mother and aunt had died of breast cancer," says Tensie. "After I was diagnosed, I had a mastectomy and chemotherapy. It was scary because I didn't know any breast cancer survivors at the time. The only women I had known who had had the disease were women in my family, and they had died.

"I became involved in a breast cancer recovery group and met women whose spouses had left them after their diagnosis. I feel so fortunate because Claude was by my side every day."

Claude admits to another challenge in their relationship, and says that if it weren't for how Tensie deals with it, they might not be together. Claude's position as head coach for boys' track and field and coach for girls' cross-country at Cleveland Heights High School frequently takes him away from home for two days at a time. As the national director for track and field for a program called "People to People Sports Ambassadors," Claude has also traveled with students internationally for two to three weeks at a time during the summer.

"People sometimes wonder if there is a husband around because I'm gone so much," explains Claude. "I feel extremely blessed that Tensie is not the kind of wife who is needy. Sometimes wives have to have their husbands with them all of the time, and when they're not, they create bad blood.

"I have to let Tensie be Tensie, allow her to have her own life, and support her in it. If it requires her to be away from me to do that, I have to give her that latitude, because she sure gives it to me."

The physical and emotional space Tensie and Claude allow each other is one of the keys to their successful marriage.

"When I come home at the end of the day, Tensie isn't up in my face with this problem or that problem," explains Claude. "I enjoy coming home. Sometimes we can sit together and not say a word, and still be communicating. That's a beautiful thing."

When Tensie is not working as a bereavement coordinator at Hospice of the Western Reserve and Claude is not working as a grade-level house coordinator at Cleveland Heights High School, they enjoy going to concerts or eating at their favorite restaurant, Phil the Fire, located near Shaker Square.

In their busy schedule, this couple always finds time to spend with one of their favorite people—and their only living parent—Claude's mother, Bernice Holland, who lives only four houses away from them.

"We just love living so close to my mother," says Claude. "People call her 'Mom Holland' because she's a mom to everybody."

Maternal instincts aside, Bernice was a trailblazer in her day by being the number-one hurdler in the U.S. indoor high jump in the 1948 Olympic Games, and at the age of 76 she has continued using her talent in track and field by being Claude's assistant track and field coach for many years.

As two people who both lost a parent at an early age, Tensie and Claude know the treasure they have in Claude's mother. Their knowledge of that comes second to only one other thing: knowing the treasure they have in each other.

Imagine That!

JAN JONES & SHELLY ARTZ

The words "Always Kiss Me Goodnight," painted on a plaque hanging in their bedroom, are a symbol of the romance Jan Jones and Shelly Artz seem to effortlessly weave into their daily existence.

More than an isolated gesture, romantic love is an attitude, a way of life. Upon entering Jan and Shelly's Moreland Hills home, it becomes obvious to me that this couple doesn't merely dabble in a romantic, imaginative lifestyle. It's in their blood. From the dangling crystal chandelier that shimmers in their foyer to the open trunk overflowing with whimsical garments and accessories that sits prominently in their living room, it is clear that Jan and Shelly take the world of romance and imagination seriously.

Being creative and imaginative comes easily to Jan. Active in theater at Mayfield High School and later as a drama major at Michigan State University, she began performing at an early age.

"I always wanted to perform, but I never thought I would go into television," says Jan.

After graduating with a degree in speech and theater, with an English and education minor, Jan was hired as a middle school teacher. While teaching, Jan became involved in community theater and was encouraged by one of the directors to audition for commercials. Having been raised by a father who owned an advertising specialties company, she knew instinctively how to sell herself. When she heard that Channel 8 was looking for a weather girl, she jumped at the chance to audition.

"I watched Dick Goddard at night and called WW1-1212 so I knew what the weather was," explains Jan. "I auditioned and had a ball. The weather map was a magnetic board and I remember tossing the sun-shaped magnet onto the board and smiling. Two days later the station called and said they wanted to hire me."

Jan's position as weather girl eventually led to her becoming the host of a talk show on Channel 8 called *Noontime*. Although the show's ratings eventually dropped and Jan's position was elimi-nated, it was on the set of *Noontime* that she first met Shelly Artz.

Shelly, who was a well-known and respected plastic surgeon, had been invited to be a guest on the show in 1976.

"I remember the day I met Jan," says Shelly. "She had a sparkle in her eye that made me feel like I was the most important per-son. Even I, who was full of myself at the time, was taken with her."

"We had a two-part segment with a commercial in between," remembers Jan. "When we started the interview, Shelly was so at ease. He had such a great sense of humor. He teased me on the air and we genuinely laughed. We had an instant rapport."

After *Noontime* was off the air, Jan didn't see Shelly again until she was hired by Channel 5 to replace Liz Richards on *The Morn-ing Exchange* in 1979.

"We had been living in our own separate worlds in between seeing each other on *Noontime* and *The Morning Exchange*," re-members Jan. "Shelly was married and I was married for a second time. When we reconnected, we felt so comfortable with each other."

"We became good friends," says Shelly. "It got to the point that whenever we saw each other, we wouldn't just talk about plastic surgery. We'd talk about our families."

In 1984, Jan left *The Morning Exchange* to move to Boston with her second husband. When she returned, her marriage ended, and she once again became a single mother.

"One of the reasons I did so well in Cleveland was that I was always working to support my kids," explains Jan. "When I wasn't working at a regular television studio job like *The Morning Exchange* or *PM Magazine*, I was doing commercials or speaking engagements. Even without child support or alimony, I was able to put my daughter through college with no loans. When you're second-generation Slovenian, you don't whine or complain. I survived two divorces, raised my children alone most of the time, and did just fine."

By the early 1990s, both Jan and Shelly were divorced and dating other people. As a television personality, Jan often had social functions to attend. In passing one day, Shelly told Jan that if she ever needed an escort to one of her functions, he would be happy to oblige.

"I remember asking Shelly to join me at one of these gatherings, as just friends," says Jan. "It's very wonderful when you fall in love with your friend. We were professional friends first, then personal friends."

Shelly and Jan are candid about the evolution of their relationship. Not only did they get to know each other as professional and personal friends, but they developed a doctor–patient relationship as well.

"Shelly did my nose," reveals Jan. Not the least bit shy about admitting that she has had "work" done, she says, "I'm 57 years old. I wouldn't look like this if I hadn't had a face lift and plastic surgery!"

Not long after Shelly and Jan began dating, Shelly faced a serious health challenge. In 1991, at the age of forty-nine, he had triple-bypass surgery.

"Shelly was a heavy smoker when he had that heart trouble," says Jan. "When we were dating and I realized we were serious about one another, I told him that I wouldn't be interested in him if he continued to smoke. I explained that I couldn't date a smoker, I couldn't kiss a smoker, and I couldn't marry a smoker."

"I quit cold turkey," says Shelly. "When you really want something, you can take control of your life."

With his smoking habit under control and a diamond ring in his pocket, Shelly decided to ask Jan to marry him while they were 35,000 feet in the air. On the way to a business trip in Flagstaff, Arizona, Shelly arranged with the captain of the airplane to announce his proposal to Jan.

"I was standing in the aisle stretching when the captain's voice came over the intercom system and said, 'This is your captain speaking. May I have your attention, please. I would just like you to know that the passenger in seat 26B would like to ask the passenger in 26A if she would marry him.' I remember screaming and saying 'Yes, yes, yes.' Everyone on the plane stood up and applauded, and the flight attendants came down the aisle with champagne. It was very fun."

On June 20, 1993, Jan and Shelly got married at a time when they were sure that all four of their children would be able to attend. The night before their wedding, they celebrated Jan's parents' 50th wedding anniversary at Landerhaven, and invited their family and close friends to join them at their home the following day for a picnic. All of the guests arrived at Shelly and Jan's the next day expecting a Sunday-afternoon barbeque, but were surprised when they realized the barbeque was really a wedding.

"No one else but our four children knew," says Jan. "We didn't want to take anything away from my parents' 50th wedding anniversary."

Shelly smiles when thinking of their secret wedding plans and says, "At the reception in our home we had a string quartet, lots of balloons, and matchbooks that said, 'Of course we're getting married today.'"

Now married for 10 years, Jan and Shelly have faced a challenge that has made their already strong marriage even stronger. Eight years after Shelly's triple-bypass surgery, he realized that his heart trouble had returned.

"The left ventricle of Shelly's heart was shot," explains Jan. "He had begun to feel weak and out of breath."

After the doctors inserted an experimental device that attached an electrode to Shelly's left ventricle, he had another two good years. At the end of two years, Shelly struggled to walk up the stairs. In November of 2002, he went to the Cleveland Clinic to be evaluated as a candidate for a heart transplant and didn't leave the hospital until March of 2003.

"Shelly lived at the Cleveland Clinic as a resident while waiting for a heart," remembers Jan. "He was attached to an IV that dripped a medicine into him to keep the heart pumping adequately. Because he was at end-stage heart failure, he would have died without that medicine."

The day LifeBanc, a national organization that searches for organs, found a heart for Shelly, the nurses came to his room to share the exciting news, but Shelly wasn't there. He was busy walking the halls.

"I wanted to be in the best shape possible so I could coast through the transplant," says Shelly.

Shelly was in good shape for the transplant, but the heart he received did not operate properly.

"It was like putting a brand-new battery into an old car, and the battery wouldn't start," explains Shelly.

Eventually, Shelly received another heart, but because of complications with bleeding, he needed five more procedures to rectify the ensuing problems. During that time, he was on life support twice.

"All through this, I was totally at peace," says Jan. "I really believed that he would make it. Even when everything went wrong, the surgeons, nurses, technicians, and staff at the Cleveland Clinic exuded hope and professionalism. I had faith."

"The reason I walk around today is because of Jan," says Shelly. "There is no question I made it because of her. She's my princess."

A small pop-up tent shaped like a castle sits in the basement for their grandchildren to enjoy. Although this couple would be hard pressed to fit into the tent, it doesn't matter. For in their imaginations, they are each other's prince and princess, and their home is truly their fairy-tale castle.

Faith First

MOSHE & ROCHEL FINE

Some would say they live an extreme lifestyle, but to Rochel and Moshe Fine, their choices in life have made perfect sense. Having both been raised in Jewish homes that were not Orthodox, they have swung the pendulum in the opposite direction for their family of seven.

"What defines someone as being an Orthodox Jew or not an Orthodox Jew is the degree to which they consider Jewish law to be binding upon them," explains Moshe, a rabbi and career consultant. "Jewish law has something to say on every aspect of life, from how you get up in the morning to how you go to bed at night, and everything in between."

It was while in law school at Southwest University School of Law in Los Angeles that Moshe became involved with an Orthodox synagogue in Venice, California. After graduating and practicing law for a time, he spent a year in Israel studying at a seminary.

Moshe returned to the United States for two weeks to celebrate Passover in April of 1994. Little did he know that by the time he boarded the plane to fly back to Israel, his life would be moving in a completely different direction.

"While out of the country, I had been corresponding with a friend in the States who I was thinking about going into business with," says Moshe. "When I came home to celebrate the holiday, my friend and his wife told me about a girl they wanted me to meet who was single, Jewish, and observant."

The girl Moshe's friends were referring to was Rochel, who at the time was living in Los Angeles and working toward a master's degree from UCLA.

"I had been visiting a girlfriend in Montreal and returned to find phone messages from my friend saying that I had to quickly call her back because she had this guy she wanted me to meet," remembers Rochel. "When I called her, she said, 'I know this guy who is a friend of my husband's and is visiting from Israel. He's a lawyer, he's cute, he's nice, he'll be an amazing husband and father, and he's leaving in five days.'"

Rochel thought her friend was crazy, but she agreed to have Moshe call her. Having taught in a Jewish private school as well as having studied in a women's seminary in Israel for one year, Rochel was aware of and prepared to follow the dating protocol of the Orthodox lifestyle.

In Orthodox Judaism, husbands and wives do not touch members of the opposite sex other than their own spouse or a close relative. When prospective partners date, not only is premarital sex out of the question, even holding hands is not allowed.

"In Judaism, the purpose of dating is not to have a good time," explains Moshe. "The purpose of dating is to get married. The courtship is structured around communication because there is nothing else. Therefore, the stage is set for a short courtship."

"I knew that when I went out with Moshe, I would be looking to see whether or not we would get married," says Rochel. "In the Orthodox lifestyle, a couple discusses everything on a date. A man or woman doesn't date for a year, while on his or her best behavior, and then all of a sudden let the other person know that he or she is moody. They discuss everything right away."

Rochel and Moshe went on two more dates before Moshe left for Israel. During that time, they discussed everything from how many children they wanted to what they were like when they got up in the morning.

Rochel remembers being very candid when describing her personality to Moshe. "I told him, 'If you're the type of person who needs your space and needs time alone, you shouldn't marry me. I am the type of person who will interrupt you 100 times and ask you 50 questions while you're sitting on the couch reading a book.' I wanted him to know that I need a lot of attention.'"

Whereas Rochel's description of herself might have made another man bolt for the door, it caused Moshe to turn to her and say, "I cannot tell you how I would love to be with someone who wants to be with me that much."

"That's when I knew Moshe was the man I wanted to marry," says Rochel.

The next day, Moshe left for Israel to finish his studies and did not return for three and a half months. During that time, the couple communicated by writing letters, phoning one another, and sending audiotapes back and forth of poems they had recited and songs they had sung.

Rochel remembers feeling nervous when she picked up Moshe from the airport on the day he returned from overseas.

"Even though we had discussed the whole world and had written back and forth and spoken for three and a half months, I hadn't seen or touched him. When Moshe got into the car, I gave him a letter to read that described my deep feelings for him. Later we bought Chinese food, went to the park, and talked until very late."

At that point in their relationship, although they had been on only four or five dates together, Moshe and Rochel were certain they wanted to be married. At three o'clock in the morning in his mother's house, Moshe blurted out the words "Marry me." Rochel responded with a quiet, but confident "Okay."

Four and a half weeks later, on August 21, 1994, Rochel and Moshe were married and began living their dream of building a home and family in accordance with their Orthodox beliefs. In line with their religious traditions, their marriage was not followed by a honeymoon, but was instead followed by seven nights of dinners.

"In Jewish tradition, the wedding ceremony is succeeded by

seven nights of dinner parties," explains Moshe. "At the end of each meal, seven special blessings are said to the bride and groom as a way to wish them a happy life together."

"After the wedding, attention is placed on the internal things in life," says Rochel. "It's not that people don't ever go away on a honeymoon, but the real focus after a couple marries is on building a home."

Although some of what this University Heights couple incorporates into their relationship may seem radical, it is what they believe has made their nine-year marriage successful.

"One of the aspects of Jewish law that distinguishes Orthodox couples from non-Orthodox couples is something called the laws of family purity," explains Moshe. "This means that during the time a woman is menstruating, the husband and wife don't have relations, nor do they sleep in the same bed. During this period we do not touch. It is a time of complete separation."

"When you are together, you are completely intimate," says Rochel. "The times that you're not together, you are completely separate. During those days, you work on communication with your spouse. You talk, spend time together, and go out on dates.

"The period that you are physically apart builds anticipation. When you do get back together, it is very special, like your wedding night all over again. It's a constant renewal of the relationship."

When Rochel and Moshe are physically apart every month, they find other ways to connect and enjoy each other's company. Because they do not have a television in their home, they read aloud to one another, play board games, or go out on dates.

"We spend so much time with each other and with our five kids because we don't have a television in our home," says Rochel. "We have dinner together every night. On Friday nights, we have special dinners when as few as five or as many as 40 may join us for a meal."

On Saturday, the Sabbath, Rochel and Moshe do not work, use the telephone, or do anything that might detract from their focus on the family. Instead, they open their home to friends, neighbors, and relatives.

Because both had parents who divorced when they were small children, Rochel and Moshe have made a pact with one another not to get divorced. The strength they find in each other and in their marriage they attribute to their way of life.

"Growing up in the Orthodox community is, to us, an idealistic lifestyle," says Moshe. "The strong sense of family and community is something we find very attractive."

Rochel feels her marriage is a testament to the Orthodox lifestyle she leads with Moshe.

"I can honestly say that my husband is my best friend. I have the most amazing marriage."

Why Wait? Do It Now

DEBBIE & MAURICE LaFOND

When you watch Debbie and Maurice LaFond together, you can't help but smile. Sitting side by side in a double rocking chair in their family room, this couple volleys quips and one-liners back and forth, kidding and prodding each other until their playful sarcasm gives way to reveal the utter devotion behind it. They are in love and have been for 28 years.

The seeds of that love were planted one February day in 1975 on an army base in Fort Campbell, Kentucky. Debbie had been a finance clerk on base and Maurice a military intelligence officer. As a favor to a friend, Maurice agreed to help Debbie move off post and into a mobile home that morning.

"We moved Debbie into a trailer that had no heat or electricity. Nobody else had good credit but me, so I was invited to stay," remembers Maurice.

Eight hours later, they both knew what they felt for each other was right. There had been a strong physical attraction, for sure. But what impressed Debbie and Maurice most was that they felt eerily comfortable in each other's presence, as though they had known one another for years.

"We were meant to find each other," says Maurice.

Three weeks later, they were engaged.

"I was only 18 and Maurice was 21 and just back from Vietnam when we met, but we've defied the statistics and have been married ever since." Debbie is convinced that the success of their against-the-odds marriage comes from a life philosophy they both share: do what you want to do, and do it *now*.

"We don't wait to do what we want to do because we realize how short a lifetime can be. I've seen too many couples spend decades waiting for the 'right time' to do something like take a cruise around the world or build a dream house, but because they wait too long, they end up getting sick or dying before they get the chance to live their dream," says Maurice.

This couple's "do it now" mentality has kept them committed to a mutual passion—sports-car racing. Although Maurice had raced cars since he was a teenager, Debbie had never been exposed to the sport. For the first two years of their marriage, she sat home while her husband raced, not wanting anything to do with it.

"Aside from the fact that Deb finally decided she wanted a chance to race, she got tired of watching me bring home broken race cars. I was much better at putting them together than I was at driving them," explains Maurice.

Debbie admits that she was itching to get behind the wheel just to see if she could do it. "I'm very competitive. I was the only girl in my family . . . and one of the few on my army base. I was a product of the women's equal rights movement, and I wanted to prove to myself that I could race with the best of them."

Maurice encouraged Debbie to take racing lessons and to overcome her initial fear of speed. And overcome it she did. She has won over 50 awards and numerous championship titles to prove it.

Rather than risk having competition come between them or damaging his ego, which was still intact, Maurice traded in his racing helmet for a toolbox and became his wife's mechanic. Little did he know that years down the road his knowledge and talent as a mechanic and member of the pit crew would save Debbie's life.

One afternoon in 1996 at Nelson Ledges racetrack, Debbie was driving her fastest time to date and spun out into the tire wall, puncturing her gas tank. Maurice watched as she turned into the pit lane and the back of her car suddenly burst into flames. Although he screamed "Fire!" into her headset, she didn't hear him.

Seeing his wife's car burning with her inside it, Maurice sprinted 50 yards and pulled her to safety in less than 25 seconds. While Debbie sat on the sidelines and let the shock waves settle, Maurice fixed her gas tank. Three hours later, one of the men from the pit crew told her that Maurice wanted her to get suited up again because the car was fixed.

"Maurice insisted the car was as good as new, and that he and the crew wouldn't ask me to race unless it was absolutely safe," remembers Debbie.

"I was impressed," adds Maurice. "Most of the male drivers there that day wouldn't have had Deb's guts and determination."

Debbie reaches for Maurice's hand. "It was my 100 percent trust in Maurice and in our marriage that put me back behind the wheel that afternoon."

This couple's commitment to sports-car racing parallels their commitment to Cleveland. Debbie's talent as a driver could take her to racetracks anywhere in the country, but the Cleveland area is where she loves to compete.

"There's good racing in Michigan, Indiana, Virginia, and Georgia, but Cleveland is where I want to be," says Debbie. "The racetracks around here are faster, with longer straightaways. Our 1,000-member club is celebrating its 50th anniversary."

When asked "What do you think your being a committed couple has done for other couples you know?" Debbie and Maurice agree on one thing: people admire them for being a demonstrative pair who are vocal about their commitment to each other.

"Being a positive role model has opened up lines of communication between us and other couples," explains Debbie. "A lot of people who are having problems start talking to us and want to know our secret for staying together."

Maurice always tells other couples that time is a resource they can't go back and recoup. "You can always get a second job. You can always make more money. You can always do other things, but you can't go back and recoup the time that you and your spouse are not together."

What Debbie and Maurice share goes much deeper than lowering track times or getting a new set of racing tires. When asked to describe Maurice in one word, Debbie chooses the word "soulful" and adds, "During racing season, we don't make it to our traditional church, but we still have church at the track. There's a deep religious connection between us."

Maurice agrees. "When I went to Vietnam, I lost a lot of religion, and I've got to be honest. Deb was one of the primary people who helped me find my way back from being the island that I thought I was. She helped me rediscover a belief and practice it."

"I figured I helped him through his recovery period from Vietnam," says Debbie. "He can help me through my change of life."

Maurice gives Debbie a skeptical glance. "What are you changing into?"

"I don't know," says Debbie. "I haven't decided yet."

Partners in Success

AMY & ARMOND BUDISH

The day Armond Budish picked up Amy Jacoby for their first date, he didn't recognize her.

"I remember Armond saying, 'You look different. Did you cut your hair?'" says Amy. "I thought that was a little odd, but didn't think much about it. After we dated for a while, Armond made a confession. He admitted that when he came to pick me up for our first date, he thought he was taking out a different girl. He had met me and a friend of mine, named Vivian, at a party. When he came to my door, he was prepared to go out with Vivian. He got me instead."

Although Armond thought he was going on a date with a different girl than the one who opened the door that day, he capitalized on the unexpected opportunity.

"On our first date, I could tell Amy had a wonderful sense of humor and was so smart," says Armond.

"One of the things I liked most about Armond was that he was oriented more toward people than material things," says Amy. "When I was on a date, I could tell more about a guy based on how he talked to a waiter, waitress, or tollbooth operator than how he talked to me. Armond always treated those who he barely knew with such respect."

In January of 1979, five months after they had started dating,

Armond proposed to Amy in the same place he had taken her for ice cream the night of their first date—a Howard Johnson's restaurant.

Amidst Formica-topped tables sporting the restaurant's famous hot dogs tucked in toasted buns, Armond transformed his reserved table into a romantic, linen-clad surface, atop of which were candlesticks and flowers.

With his props in place, Armond seized the moment and asked Amy for her hand in marriage, but instead of saying "Will you marry me?" he slipped her a note.

"I wrote out the proposal so I wouldn't mess it up," admits Armond.

"He was so nervous he broke out in a rash," remembers Amy.

"I knew Amy was the right person for me, but I was nervous," says Armond. "I was making a major decision."

Amy took the proposal as seriously as Armond, so much so that she waited until the next day to give him an answer.

"I knew I was going to say 'Yes,' but I couldn't get the words out at the exact moment," says Amy. "So, instead, I told him I needed time to think about it. He's never forgiven me for that act of procrastination!"

Amy accepted Armond's proposal the following morning, and seven months later, on August 26, 1979, they were wed, with over 100 friends and family members in attendance. After spending their wedding night at—you guessed it—Howard Johnson's Motor Lodge, Armond and Amy traveled to Massachusetts for their honeymoon.

Later that year they moved to Cleveland from Washington, D.C. Amy, originally from Long Island, had earned a bachelor's degree in community service education from Cornell University and a master's degree in consumer education from the University of Maryland. Armond, a native Clevelander, had earned a law degree from New York University.

After returning to Cleveland, Armond wanted not only to practice corporate law, but also to provide some kind of community service. He and Amy brainstormed ways to use his expertise.

The first of many ideas came with the suggestion that Armond write a weekly column in the *Plain Dealer* called "You and the Law," which made its debut in 1981 and continues to run weekly.

"The column explains how the law affects all of us, and it provides useful tips and advice on a wide range of topics," says Armond. "A number of the stories I wrote were on subjects relating to older people, such as Social Security and Medicare. Those columns always got a tremendous response. Whenever I wrote about long-term care, people wanted more information on legal issues having to do with Medicaid and how to protect assets."

After doing some research, Armond discovered there wasn't much information available on long-term care issues, so he decided to write a book on the topic. In 1986, he wrote *Avoiding the Medicaid Trap*, followed by another book, which he co-wrote with Amy in 1992, called *Golden Opportunities* (both books published by Henry Holt & Co.).

"Amy has been a true partner in all that I do," says Armond. "She is more than a cheerleader. She did a lot of the writing on both books and edits all of my newspaper and *Family Circle* magazine columns."

Amy helps Armond not only with his writing, but with his television show, also called *Golden Opportunities*. A program geared toward topics for men and women over the age of 50, it airs weekly on WKYC Channel 3.

"Amy contributes story ideas and edits the entire show," explains Armond. "She goes over all of the questions and answers for each segment. She is equal to a producer."

Although to some people it might appear as if Amy's life revolves around Armond's professional career, neither she nor Armond view it that way.

"Amy has had a number of independent-of-Armond-Budish positions," asserts Armond. "She's worked in the White House with President Carter's special assistant for consumer affairs. When we first moved back to Cleveland, she worked for Senator Metzenbaum, and she ran Lee Fisher's first district office when he was state senator. She is active in numerous Jewish communal organizations, such as the National Council of Jewish Women and the Jewish Community Federation."

"There was a time when some of my more feminist friends thought I had sold out because I was the stay-at-home mom," says Amy. "On the surface, it may appear that I don't do anything for myself, but actually, I undertake numerous other activities, one of which is taking complex materials and making them consumer friendly. Over the years, my interests and Armond's have dovetailed in a very nice way."

This Beachwood couple is as much a team on the domestic front as professionally. Parents of two sons, Ryan and Daniel, Amy and Armond remember facing the challenge of having an ill newborn.

A few days after their son Ryan was born, he began projectile vomiting and losing weight, until his weight dropped to three pounds.

"We were terrified," remembers Armond. "Although the doctors eventually diagnosed the problem as pyloric stenosis, we lived for days watching our son's health decline."

Amy remembers spending sleepless nights in the hospital by her son's crib. "We would sit up all night playing cards together because we were afraid that if we didn't stay awake and keep watch, Ryan would aspirate the vomit and choke to death."

This couple's fear nearly became a reality.

"One night I was sitting next to Ryan's hospital crib reading the paper when out of the corner of my eye, I saw his arms and legs flailing," recalls Armond. "He was turning blue. He had aspirated his vomit because a nurse had placed him on his back. If not for me being there to pick him up, Ryan could have choked to death."

Married 24 years, this couple has strong opinions on the meaning of commitment in a marriage.

"Every day you could probably think of 10 good reasons why you should divorce the person you're married to," says Amy, "but, instead, you have to wake up each morning with the assumption that you want to be married."

"I think it's good for children to not only see their parents work together, but play together," says Armond.

One of the things Armond and Amy appreciate most about their relationship is each other's sense of humor. Known to be a practical joker, Armond enjoys being silly.

"By the time the weekend rolls around, Armond is tired of talking seriously," says Amy. "We understand each other's humor. When I make a joke, Armond gets it."

Armond leans over and kisses Amy. "I love my wife," he says. And that's no joke.

Making it Work, Together

LIZ & MICHAEL SYMON

As a chef, Michael Symon is passionate, enthusiastic, and completely committed. As a husband, he is no different. It doesn't take more than five minutes of being in Michael and Liz's presence, or a look at Michael's motorcycle, to realize how much he adores his wife. Although a likeness of Liz is painted on the side of Michael's Harley, the true indicator of how much he respects and admires her is the way he looks at her.

Before meeting Michael in 1990, Liz had worked in the restaurant business in Boston as a server and private party manager, and then at Players restaurant in Lakewood, Ohio.

"Michael had just finished at the Culinary Institute of America in Hyde Park, New York, when he applied for a position at Players," remembers Liz. "The owner of the restaurant really liked Michael and hired him. Before I met him, I had heard he was cute."

"That's when I was still cute, which was 40 pounds and a full head of hair ago," says Michael before letting out a wild, runaway laugh that has become as much his trademark as has his macaroni and cheese dish.

Michael and Liz worked together at Players for two years, he as a chef and she as a manager, until Michael left and began work-

ing as a chef at Piccolo Mondo, then at Giovanni's, and finally as
the chef and general manager at the Caxton Café.

"I begged Liz to come work with me because I needed someone to manage the front of the house," says Michael.

After a year of working side by side at the Caxton Café, Liz and
Michael went out together one night after closing. Although they
had been good friends for five years, and had known a lot about
each other's personal lives, they had never viewed their relationship as more than a close friendship. Until that night.

As hard as they tried, neither one could deny the physical
chemistry and budding romance between them.

"We went out after work this one time and stuff started happening," remembers Michael. "We both looked at each other and
said, 'Uh, oh. That can't happen again. That was bad. We've been
friends for all this time. If we keep doing this, we'll screw up our
friendship.'"

"Some of our friends who knew we were becoming romanti-
cally involved didn't think it was a good idea," says Liz. "But when
we had a meeting with the owners of the Caxton Café to tell them
we were involved with each other, they were really good about it."

Michael and Liz had every reason to feel confident about their
ability to be in a romantic relationship and still maintain professionalism at work. Having worked together on and off for five
years prior to their positions at the Caxton Café, they were used
to slipping into defined roles.

Liz has a theory as to why she and Michael work so well together.

"A lot of people who get involved and decide to go into business together sometimes find it doesn't work because they haven't
been used to being around each other a lot. We were used to being
together all of the time."

With a five-year friendship as a foundation, Liz and Michael
dated for one more year before becoming engaged, and waited
two and a half more years before getting married in 1998. A year
before, they brought into the world what they now look upon as
their baby. Her name is Lola.

When considering what to call their restaurant, Michael wanted the name to be short, and Liz wanted it to sound feminine. "The concept for the restaurant was to be curvy and sexy," explains Liz. "When Michael said the name 'Lola,' I said, 'That's perfect! That's exactly what our child should be named.'"

Lola Bistro & Wine Bar is now seven years old, and as owners, Liz and Michael admit to having different management styles. One of the sticking points between them is the difference in how each of them approaches their staff.

"I'm more lenient," says Liz. "I'm very nonconfrontational when it comes to the staff, where Michael is much more forceful."

Michael agrees with Liz. "There are two ways. The wrong way and my way. I have to do the dirty work. Lizzy coddles and I do the firing, although in seven years, I've only fired two employees."

Liz and Michael work equally hard at running their restaurant, with Michael handling what goes on in the kitchen and Liz dealing with the books and the front of the house. When they receive media coverage, which happens often, their division of labor is sometimes misrepresented. For Liz and Michael, that's frustrating.

"When reviewers write about restaurants, they tend to latch on to chefs," explains Michael. "Often a review will say 'Michael Symon's Lola or Michael this or Michael that.' It has never built animosity between us, but it's still been a hard thing."

"It was really difficult for me in the beginning," says Liz, "because I'd work, and work, and work, and then a lot of the time, I'd be eliminated from the review."

Although Liz appreciates being included when there is recognition of the restaurant's success, when the media wants to highlight Michael as a chef, she is first in line to applaud her husband.

"Nineteen ninety-eight was a big year," says Liz. "Michael won *Food & Wine* magazine's top 10 best chefs in the country. Soon after, he began making guest appearances on the Food Network's show called *Ready, Set, Cook,* and then in 1999, he was asked to cohost his own show on the Food Network, called *The Melting Pot.*"

Each week, from Tuesday through Sunday, Michael and Liz

work between 40 and 60 hours. On the days when Liz works fewer hours than Michael, it is because she is spending time with Kyle, her teenage son from a previous marriage.

When not in the kitchen or dining room, Michael and Liz are on the second floor of the restaurant, either catering a private party or teaching cooking classes.

"We offer two types of cooking classes," says Liz. "We do a basic technique class, where the topic might be about stews or roasting. The other class teaches how to cook a five-course meal based on a cultural theme."

Because so much of their time is spent running the restaurant, you wouldn't think this Brook Park couple would find time for romance, but they do.

"We're spoiled," says Michael. "We have a pretty romantic lifestyle in the sense that we're always around people who are celebrating romantic events and are in the restaurant for special occasions."

Although many of their business-related trips to Napa Valley have ranked high on the romantic memory meter, they agree that their most romantic memory is of New Year's Eve 2001.

"It was the first New Year's Eve we had taken off from the restaurant," explains Michael. "I brought home these beautiful, big, fresh crab legs, and a bottle of champagne."

"We sat on the floor in front of the fire and enjoyed what was probably the best dinner we had ever eaten," says Liz.

Although this couple does not share the same taste in music or leisure activities—Michael listens to heavy metal and enjoys football while Liz likes cultural activities and enjoys any type of music except heavy metal—they are identical when it comes to their taste buds.

"If I like the way something tastes, Liz will like the way something tastes and vice versa," says Michael. "If she loves a wine, I'll taste it and love it too. From a palate standpoint, we are so similar."

That similarity has helped shape this couple's success story and eventually led them to be featured in Michael Ruhlman's best-selling book *The Soul of a Chef* (Viking, 2000). One-third of this book, which is mandatory reading for students in culinary schools across the nation, is devoted to the evolution of Lola Bistro & Wine Bar. At one point in the text, the author refers to one of the restaurant's particularly profitable evenings.

"Twenty-five hundred dollars' worth of food has just been ordered and cooked between nine and ten. It is Lola's most lucrative hour ever. But it is too much. Liz arrives to see how Michael's doing; she knows he's had a hard time, so she doesn't say anything, just lets him talk . . . The evening doesn't end there. It's only half over . . . Frank, Matt, and Abby still cooking hard, the bar packed, and tables filling up *again* for dinner. At one in the morning. In Cleveland. This does not happen in Cleveland."

On the contrary. Thanks to one couple's commitment—to each other and to a shared vision—it does now.

Spiritual Bedrock

THERESA & GREG JOHNSON

"I believe she is here for a purpose," says Greg of his wife, Theresa. "I build her up and push her to be more than she has ever been. Theresa is Pueblo Indian. She tries to downplay it, but I won't let her do that."

Although Theresa doesn't broadcast it, her heritage is important to her, for she feels it is her connection to everything.

"I carry the spirits of my ancestors with me," explains Theresa. "I believe we are connected to all things. The earth, the plants, and the animals. When I see an animal, I see my brother or sister."

Greg admits that when he first noticed Theresa in 1996 while speaking at a small conference for the Urban League in Colorado Springs, he was attracted to her physical beauty. After he met Theresa and got to know her, it was her spiritual nature that he found most appealing.

As an audience member at the Urban League conference, Theresa was captivated by Greg's stage presence. After Greg finished speaking, he and Theresa spoke briefly.

"Whether he is speaking to a crowd or sitting at a table with a group of people, Greg has a powerful persona," says Theresa. "As soon as he started talking at the conference, I began listening to what he had to say."

Before returning to Cleveland the next day, Greg left his name, address, and phone number for Theresa at the hotel's front desk. Instead of receiving a call from Theresa, Greg received a call from a male colleague who had been at the conference and had exchanged business cards with Theresa. The man had contacted Greg for the sole purpose of suggesting that he call Theresa. Although to this day neither Greg nor Theresa understands why a colleague took the time to encourage Greg to call her, they will be forever grateful that he did.

"Our first dates were long-distance phone dates between Cleveland and Denver," remembers Greg. "We talked about everything and anything."

Their next face-to-face meeting after having met at the conference in Colorado Springs occurred when Greg went to Theresa's home in Denver to offer his support when she had an operation. Afterwards, it was a visit to Cleveland and a decision not to take a job in Arizona that led Theresa to move to Cleveland and live with Greg and his son, Gregory Quentin Brandon Johnson, who they affectionately called GQ.

On November 28, 1998, an unusually balmy day with the temperature reaching 70 degrees, Theresa and Greg got married in Cleveland on the *Nautica Queen*.

"We wanted to have our wedding on the water," says Theresa. "During our reception, Santa Claus ran alongside the boat on a jet ski, and the Cleveland Fire Department squirted us as they went by."

Less than two years into their marriage, this couple suffered a profound loss, the loss of Greg's son, GQ. At the age of 17, GQ was diagnosed with diabetes.

"There were times he would be sitting around with us and black out," remembers Greg. "He was so sick. Theresa took better care of him than anyone."

"I remember him wanting to play basketball, but not having the strength to play," says Theresa.

"Contracting diabetes as a teenager is the worst," says Greg.

"All of a sudden when someone tells you that you can't do this, this, this, and this, it feels like you have to live in a glass bubble."

Hospitalized several times during the course of his disease, GQ passed away at home on September 20, 1999.

"He had been ill over the weekend," recalls Greg. "The day he passed away, Theresa had spoken with him before going to work. As usual, I was working out of our house. When I checked on him that morning, he was gone.

"GQ is my first thought every day and my last thought every day. He was a major part of our lives."

"He is with us a lot," says Theresa. "It's no different than the ancestors we carry with us all the time."

One of the things that helped Theresa and Greg get through the loss of GQ was their connection to nature. The day GQ died, Greg felt his son's spirit in the flight of birds.

"Within an hour after GQ died, the tree across the street from our house had no fewer than one hundred crows in it," says Greg. "Shortly after seeing the crows, I went to a spot in the Metropark where several of them had lighted in another tree. Along with the crows sat what looked like a hawk. I remember watching the birds and talking to GQ. Suddenly the hawk flew away, surrounded by a circle of crows. In my mind, the hawk flying away was my son's spirit leaving, and the crows were his guides."

Theresa and Greg agree that GQ's passing gave Greg the mission of finishing something he had started before his son died. That something was a fatherhood initiative called "I Am a Dream," the goal of which is to produce newsletters, workshops, seminars, and conferences to strengthen the role of fathers in the life of children, families, and the community.

"We had no sponsorship for last year's conference," explains Greg. "People kept saying we wouldn't be able to pull it off, but we did it. We had over 140 people at the conference, many from Florida, Michigan, and New York. The city council, as well as the board of education, gave us a proclamation of support."

Both Greg and Theresa are active in the fatherhood initiative.

Greg puts much of his energy into the production of newsletters and the organization of annual conferences. For the past two years, Theresa has contributed by working with women to help them realize the importance of the father's role in the family.

"Females can't be fathers," insists Theresa. "Trying to raise a family without the participation of a father takes a huge toll on a woman."

Throughout their four-year marriage, Theresa and Greg's relationship has grown deeper with each passing day. This Cleveland couple agrees that more than love, respect is the cornerstone of a solid, lifelong marriage.

"Respect is more important than that other elusive thing we call love," says Greg. "I don't even know what that love thing means. For me, love is an emotion that goes up and down. Respect is really the foundation of any relationship."

Greg feels strongly that husbands and wives need to appreciate each other not only for who they are, but also for what they are put on this earth to do.

"Theresa has the larger mission in life of shaping the character and future of children everywhere. She's reluctant to pursue that mission, but I won't let her forget about it. We're just waiting for the right opportunity to come along."

Without a doubt, mutual support and respect have helped create the bedrock upon which this couple's marriage has been built, but what keeps the foundation airtight and fracture-free is their belief that everything in life has a spiritual connection.

"Spirituality is the overarching thing in our relationship," says Greg. " We're on a journey. We walk a path set by someone larger than us."

"Our spirituality has deepened our bond," says Theresa. "It never goes away. It lasts forever."

A Lifetime Guarantee

DOROTHY & REUBEN SILVER

When you meet Dorothy and Reuben Silver and hear this Cleveland Heights couple talk about their latest project, you realize that you've had the honor and pleasure of discovering their mutual passion: theater.

They were both children when they fell head over heels in love with the world of performance, Dorothy as an usher at a theater and Reuben as a student in a Jewish cultural school. It was then that each of them began a lifelong affair with the stage.

"When I was 13 years old, I began to usher at the Cass Theater in downtown Detroit," remembers Dorothy. "I watched plays on Saturday afternoons and was fascinated with everything about the theater. What I enjoyed most was observing a person becoming someone other than who he or she was in real life. To step into someone else's shoes means you have to understand and acquire empathy for that person."

When Dorothy thinks about her ability to take on the role of a character, she gives credit to her dramatic family.

"My relatives were not discreet about their feelings or opinions," explains Dorothy. "They waved their arms, yelled, cried, and slammed doors. It was wonderful. They were people who had strong feelings and weren't afraid to reveal them."

As an eight-year-old student in a Jewish cultural school in Detroit, Reuben entered a Yiddish-language drama program. In 1933, flourishing Jewish theaters would host touring companies from New York. When the touring company needed children for a production, a talent scout would be sent ahead to audition child actors for the show. Reuben was one of those actors.

"I was performing plays at the age of eight in Detroit with many of the big names of the Yiddish-language theater," says Reuben. "I could either play children my own age or 90-year-old Old Testament prophets. I now understand how the Yiddish-language theater impacted my taste and formed my dramatic style."

With the love of theater coursing through their veins, it was no surprise that Reuben and Dorothy would be drawn to performing at Wayne State University in Detroit in the late '40s (when it was known as Wayne University). Whenever each of them wasn't working to earn money, Reuben as a cab driver and Dorothy as a secretary, they were doing what they loved doing most—acting onstage.

"I remember seeing this girl performing at Wayne University in a Tennessee Williams one-act play," says Reuben. "Although she was brand new there, she was a pretty good actress."

"I knew who Reuben was," says Dorothy, "because he was prominent in the Detroit theater scene. He came up to me one day and asked me to go out for coffee with him.

"By that point, I had met a succession of young men who were on their way to stable, professional careers, and they bored me to death. Suddenly, there was Reuben. First of all, he was in the theater, and that had a certain cachet. Secondly, he was, and still is, a totally open person who doesn't censor himself about anything. I remember sitting in Reuben's cab when he said, 'I'm going to tell you everything about myself.' And he did. He was the first guy I had ever met who could talk like that."

The other thing Dorothy loved about Reuben was that he didn't fixate on her appearance. As a young woman, she had earned money by selling dresses in women's clothing stores and often watched men choose their wives' clothing.

"I thought it was awful for women to be pirouetting in front of their husbands, who then decided whether or not they should buy the dress," says Dorothy. "When I ask Reuben, 'How do I look?' before we go out, he looks at my face. He doesn't ask me to twirl around and display parts of me. He looks at me, at my eyes, and says, 'I think you look great.'"

"For me, the ideal woman had to have brains and talent," says Reuben. "Dorothy is certainly good-looking, but looks were not at the top of my list."

The only thing below physical appearance on Reuben's priority list was marriage. Although undoubtedly a couple for many months, Reuben and Dorothy had never talked about marriage. So, when Reuben called Dorothy on the phone and suggested they become husband and wife, she was taken aback.

"I was on a family vacation in Mexico City when I received an eight-page telegram from my closest English professor, my mentor, from Wayne University," recalls Reuben. "He contacted me because he had learned about a position at the University of Connecticut that he thought I would be perfect for. It was a graduate program that would give me the opportunity to earn a master's degree, teach, and work in the theater. I called Dorothy from Mexico City to read her the telegram and said, 'Do you think we could get married?' To this day, I don't know how that came out of my mouth. All I knew was that I wanted to spend the rest of my life with her."

After a small wedding held in their rabbi's home in 1949, Dorothy and Reuben packed up their belongings and headed to Storrs, Connecticut. Over the next several years, they traveled around the country acting and directing at university, professional, and community theaters and in summer stock until they settled in Columbus, where Reuben worked to earn his Ph.D. in theater at Ohio State University.

"That was the time in history when men earned graduate degrees and women earned a 'Ph.T.,' which stood for 'Putting Hubby Through,'" says Dorothy. "Back then women worked to help their husbands get through school so that they could become the main wage earner. I never questioned that. While I was supporting Reuben as he worked toward his Ph.D., he was enormously encouraging to me while I worked, raised our three boys, and pursued my own theater career."

Reuben had completed everything he needed to earn his Ph.D. except for his dissertation when he learned of a job opening in Cleveland as artistic director at Karamu Theater.

"When I called Karamu to see if they were still searching for a director, I was told that Mr. and Mrs. Jelliffe, the founders of Karamu Theater, were in New York looking for someone to fill the position," recalls Reuben. "I hung up the phone in Columbus, looked at Dorothy, and said, 'The streets of New York are crawling with theater directors. What chance would we have?' Dorothy said, 'If you want the job, you've got to apply.'"

After reviewing Reuben's application, the Jelliffes traveled to Columbus to interview him and Dorothy. After a second interview with the Jelliffes and their staff in Cleveland, Reuben was offered the job at a starting salary of $4,800 a year.

"I was there for 21 years, from 1955 to 1976, and was very, very happy," says Reuben.

While Reuben worked as the artistic director at Karamu, Dorothy made a matching contribution there as an actress, assistant director, and resident guest director. Since leaving Karamu in 1976, the Silvers have bestowed upon Cleveland their performing and directorial talents in a variety of theaters, such as the Cleveland State University Factory Theater, the Dobama Theater, Ensemble Theater, the Great Lakes Shakespeare Festival, and the Beck Center for the Arts.

When asked what commitment in a marriage means to them, Dorothy and Reuben compare it to their commitment to the theater.

"If you don't commit yourself to a marriage fully, then you're not really testing if it will work," says Reuben. "It's the same as when kids used to come to me when I was a college advisor and say that they wanted to do theater, but wanted to take a math degree just in case. The trouble is, if a student spends time on something to back up the theater degree, he or she isn't developing the theater pursuit. It's better for a student to pursue theater fully and if it doesn't work, he or she can give it up and do the other thing."

"We don't revile people who get divorced," says Dorothy, "It's just that our whole orientation is different. Marriage is a final commitment. I've given Reuben a lifetime guarantee on me."

There are no guarantees in life, but with 54 years of matrimony behind them, this couple's commitment to each other is the exception.

I Do, I Do, I Do

DEBBIE & BILL CURRIN

Getting married more than once in our society is not unusual, so when Bill and Debbie Currin told me they had both been married three times, I was surprised, but not shocked. What shocked me was learning they had married *each other* three times.

The difference between this couple and most couples who remarry each other is that this couple never got divorced in between their wedding ceremonies. Each time they spoke their vows, it was to recommit to the strong, solid marriage they already had.

"I think commitment needs to be broken down into phases," says Debbie. "But it was Bill's idea to recommit after three years of marriage. At the time, we were entering the stage in our marriage where we wanted children."

"Up until that point, we had traveled and had really gotten to know each other," says Bill. "I knew life was going to change, so I thought before we had children, we should reset our goals and recommit ourselves to each other and our marriage."

Prior to exchanging their second set of wedding vows, Debbie and Bill made the traditional appointment with a minister as if they were newlyweds. Bill even went so far as to re-propose to Debbie.

"I didn't have another ring the second time, but I did kneel down like I had the first time around," explains Bill.

Twenty-seven years later, on their thirty-year anniversary, this couple went back to the altar. After their children left home, a time when many husbands and wives feel like strangers to each other, Debbie and Bill felt closer than ever.

"Becoming an empty-nester can be a harsh time for a husband and wife," says Debbie. "When all of a sudden it's just the two of you again, it's tough if you've forgotten to take time to know each other over the years. So that wouldn't happen to us, we made sure we went away for a week by ourselves every year. The first time we left, our daughter, Kristen, was only 10 months old. We felt that we had to keep our relationship strong or our children wouldn't have anything."

With every recommitment, the proposals became more and more romantic. Although Bill's first proposal to Debbie was in her apartment after seeing the Broadway show *I Do, I Do* with the music from the show playing in the background, his third proposal rivaled his first.

"We were in a meadow in England," remembers Debbie. "We were enjoying a picnic lunch under a great, big, beautiful tree and watching sheep wander by when Bill re-proposed to me."

"I looked at Debbie and said that because our last daughter, Bethany, was about to graduate from high school and we would soon have a new life with just the two of us again, I wanted to recommit my love to her," recalls Bill.

This couple's forward-looking approach grew from a relationship that evolved slowly and methodically. From their first date at Otterbein College to the time when Bill gave Debbie the ring three years later, they both felt the momentum increasing in their relationship.

"It was like constructing a house," says Debbie. "I felt we had a firm, solid foundation that we could build the rest of our lives upon."

Bill and Debbie agree that the foundation they laid for their marriage was and still is based on unconditional support for whatever they've chosen to do in life. Debbie has championed

Bill's involvement in their community as a city councilman, school board member, and now as the mayor of Hudson. Bill backed Debbie's entrepreneurial spirit and talent as an artist who owned a retail business for many years.

"For me, there has always been a connection to Bill beyond the fact that he is handsome and fun to be with," explains Debbie. "Bill has never played mind games like some of the other guys I dated. He has always been very emotionally mature and up front. Discussions are honest and out in the open. That is one of his great strengths, not just in our marriage, but in his work in the community, and as a father."

"When somebody makes you feel as good as Debbie makes me feel and supports your self-confidence and your esprit de corps, you can't help but be attracted to that person," says Bill.

Although the couple's mutual admiration has long been a springboard for supportive behavior toward one another, Bill admits that there was a time when he wasn't as encouraging to Debbie as he could have been.

"After our girls were born, there was a point in our marriage when I was putting an awful lot of pressure on Debbie to lose weight," remembers Bill. "My mind was being influenced by what the media was saying everyone should look like. I finally realized the problem wasn't Debbie's. It was mine. I needed to love Debbie for the woman she was, not the woman I wanted her to be. She is as beautiful today as the first day I met her."

That first day Bill met Debbie was in March of 1965. Both on spring break at Otterbein College, they shared a booth with two other friends at a campus restaurant called Ruthie's.

"The instant I met Bill, I felt a synergy between us," remembers Debbie.

"I thought Debbie was drop-dead cute," recalls Bill. "I was almost speechless."

Their meal at Ruthie's led Debbie to invite Bill to the Sadie Hawkins dance, which led Bill to invite Debbie to an Eisley Brothers concert. Although they couldn't agree on which of those events was their very first date, they did agree that the day I interviewed them was the 38th anniversary of the first time they went out alone together.

Married 35 years, this Hudson couple has lived in the same house and same city for 33 of those 35 years. During that time mutual respect has been the cornerstone of their relationship.

"Bill shows me respect daily in little ways," says Debbie. "He still opens the car door, pulls out my chair, and stands up when I come into the room. What woman doesn't feel wonderful when she has that kind of respect?"

"I think of all the support Debbie has given me over the years," adds Bill. "When you have someone who is so dedicated to you, you can't throw that aside."

When Debbie and Bill lost their home to a fire recently, they leaned on each other for, you guessed it, support.

"I was out of town when our house caught on fire," says Bill. "As soon as I came home, we drove to our other house in Chautauqua, New York, and discussed how we were going to work together to get through the whole thing."

Although this couple's successful marriage can be attributed mostly to hard work, they insist that luck has played a small part in their destiny, a belief reflected in two words they like to use.

"We have this thing we say to each other," reveals Debbie. "Sometimes when we say, 'I love you,' we add, 'I won.'"

This couple's feeling of good fortune isn't about winning prizes or the lottery, but the gift they feel they have "won" in each other.

When News Met Sports

KRISTIN & JOHN ANDERSON

To a lot of people, being a television anchor may seem like a glamorous job. It has its benefits, to be sure, but if you are a television anchor married to a television anchor, the job can have its drawbacks.

For John and Kristin Anderson, working different shifts at WKYC Channel 3 is the biggest obstacle they face as a married couple.

"I always joke that when John is working the morning show, I'm only married Saturday and half of Sunday," remarks Kristin, "because we really don't have time to be married during the week."

"When I do the morning show, I wake up at ten o'clock at night and see Kristin for an hour before I leave," says John. "When I come home, we see each other for about five hours, but between working out at the health club and Kristin getting ready for work, we only get about a half hour to talk at lunch."

Because their careers often take them in opposite directions during the week, Kristin and John are inseparable on the weekends.

"We used to run errands and go grocery shopping on Sundays but finally decided not to get bogged down with household stuff because we only have those two days together," explains John.

When John and Kristin are lucky enough to work the same

shift, people ask them how they can stand being together all of the time.

"I tell them I love every minute of it," says John.

"The first week we were on the same shift together, I told John I was falling in love with him all over again," says Kristin.

When Kristin first fell in love with John, she was 21 and he was 28. They both worked at KSTP, the ABC affiliate station in Minneapolis, where John was a sports producer and Kristin was an intern.

"I remember meeting John like it was yesterday," says Kristin. "It was a Tuesday and I was sitting at the assignment desk. I thought I had met everybody, but then I remember watching John walk by and thinking, *Who is that?*"

"I'll never forget the first day I laid eyes on her," says John. "I had just told my roommate the day before that I was done with dating. Then I saw Kristin."

John admits to having been sneaky by talking to another employee at the assignment desk just so he could get the chance to talk to Kristin.

"I remember another intern at the station telling me that John never came up to the assignment desk," says Kristin. "That was my first clue that he might be interested in me."

"Guilty," admits John. "I had no reason to be up there. We were in sports. We were always in the back of the office."

As a way to spend time together on the job, John and Kristin would volunteer to pick up dinner orders for people in the newsroom. The regular restaurant run was something they enjoyed doing together each night.

"At first we were just friends," explains Kristin. "In my mind, I kept thinking there was no way someone that high up in their career would even think about dating an intern."

"As we got to know each other, our relationship really took off," recalls John. "Our first date was 14 hours long. We played miniature golf, saw a three-hour movie, had dinner at a restaurant, and walked around a lake for the last three hours."

That 14-hour date turned into a nine-month courtship, and

then distance introduced itself into their relationship for the first time. After her internship, Kristin landed a job three hours away in Wisconsin. So that he could be closer to Kristin, John followed her a year later and took a job in news, even though it was in a smaller television market than he was used to.

After 12 months, Kristin moved again, this time even farther away.

"Kristin was determined to give the business a chance," explains John. "I was determined not to get in the way, but I wasn't going to let her go easily."

While Kristin was in Green Bay, Wisconsin, John accepted a job offer in Omaha, Nebraska. Satisfied that he would be in a larger television market that provided more stability, he decided the time had come to talk marriage. Two days after the new job offer, John proposed to Kristin.

They were in a state park situated on a bluff overlooking a valley in La Crosse, Wisconsin. As they sat side by side on a picnic bench, John turned to Kristin and began his proposal speech.

"All of a sudden I heard this noise in the background," remembers John. "I looked over and some guy was mowing the lawn. He drove right by us just as I was about to propose. No sooner had I started my speech for the second time than this same guy drove by again going the other way."

"That day I noticed John wasn't his relaxed self," recalls Kristin. "I thought he was on edge because of moving to a bigger city and having more responsibilities. I knew something was different about him, but I didn't think he was going to ask me to marry him."

Finally, the lawn mower guy left them alone, and John was able to propose. He got down on one knee, grabbed Kristin's hand, and said, "I can't imagine going to Omaha without you."

Kristin smiles at the memory. "I think I said 'yes' six times."

Married on an October morning, they had a lunchtime reception with family and friends, hopped on a plane to San Francisco, and spent their honeymoon in Napa Valley.

After three years in Omaha, John and Kristin came to Cleveland in September of 2000. They have worked opposite shifts at Channel 3 except for six months when they coanchored the news desk. As coanchors, competition between them was never an issue.

"I have a strange personality that is probably very rare in this business," admits Kristin. "For some reason, I don't want to be in the spotlight. Because of that, I have no problem turning it over to John. I could tell from some of the viewer e-mails that people saw me as submissive. It was completely not about that."

John may enjoy the spotlight, but he is very protective of his wife.

"I don't know why, but I always have this feeling of wanting to protect Kristin, no matter what," admits John. "I know it sounds like a cliché, but you could take away everything in my life, just don't take her away."

John and Kristin appreciate each other more than ever because extended time together is so rare. Working opposite shifts has forced them to learn to stay in touch in a variety of ways.

Kristin becomes emotional as she describes a particularly difficult time for the couple.

"It was the first day John had to go in to the morning show by himself. That was hard for us," says Kristin, as she wipes a tear from the corner of her eye. "I'll never forget how John slipped a card under the door for me before he left that day."

"For people who have to work opposite shifts, my best advice to them is to stay in contact," suggests John. "Write notes. When we work opposite shifts, we go through a lot of paper and pens. For the first five or six years of our relationship we didn't have cell phones. For a time there, we would write a note no matter what we were doing, even if it was just to say, 'I love you and miss you.'"

Married six years, this couple still acts like newlyweds. As they have their photograph taken in the newsroom for this book, hoots and hollers come from coworkers. "Oh, how romantic!" they shout, as John and Kristin cuddle up together behind the news desk.

They take the friendly jeers in stride. What does it matter? After all, they are together.

Age Makes No Difference

STEPHANIE MORRISON-HRBEK
& GEORGE HRBEK

When George first met Stephanie in 1967, the thought of marrying her never entered his mind. Understandably so, for Stephanie was 13 years old at the time, and George was in his mid-thirties. No one would have thought their first meeting would eventually lead to a mature, committed relationship nine years later.

In 1971, George, along with his wife and family, moved from Chicago to Cleveland so that he could continue his career as a Lutheran pastor at the Lutheran Metropolitan Ministry.

Over the years, Stephanie's sister, who had done an internship with George while working on a civil rights project in Chicago, occasionally invited George and his family to join her and her family on her mother's farm in Virginia. At one particular family gathering, George noticed Stephanie in a new way—as an adult. At this point, her family had known him for 10 years because of his involvement in social ministry.

"George was a larger-than-life guy who was very charismatic," remembers Stephanie. "So to be noticed by him felt like a big deal.

"To this day, what it was that attracted George to me remains a mystery. I think he was intrigued by the fact that I was fun and very theatrical."

When George and Stephanie met as adults, they were both at a low point in their lives.

"Although I had a college degree, I was still seeking definition in my life," recalls Stephanie. "I was an unevolved 22-year-old."

Married at the time, George was feeling confused about his life and his relationship with his wife. When Stephanie and George met as adults, they had not planned on falling in love. Their decision to be together was a joint one and was not made hastily.

"It was the beginning of painful times," remembers George. "Because of the circumstances, Stephanie and I kept reexamining and discussing the idea of us being with one another."

The process of deciding to marry each other was a distressing one for this couple and included deep discussions about George leaving his marriage.

"We had two wedding ceremonies," explains Stephanie, "one in my parents' church in East Lansing, Michigan, and one in Cleveland. During both ceremonies, we owned the fact that we were being married in the midst of brokenness. That was named."

Now, 25 years later, Stephanie and George are filled with gratitude for the integrity and grace with which everyone involved handled the situation.

"Because my former spouse is a remarkable person," says George, "we have maintained a friendship, initially meeting to discuss parenting issues around our four children. Still today, we occasionally celebrate holidays and other special events as one family."

Because of their circumstances, intense discussions replaced a traditional wedding proposal. George admits to making the idea of marrying him a bit more alluring by dangling a carrot in front of Stephanie.

"Whenever anyone asks me how I proposed to Stephanie, I say I told her that if she married me, I'd give her a theater," says George.

He fulfilled his promise.

When George moved from Chicago to Cleveland, he fell in love with the Near West Side neighborhood where he and Stephanie still live today.

"I moved to Ohio City because of the culture, hospitality, and diversity in the area," explains George.

Unfortunately, George not only discovered a positive aspect to the intriguing Near West Side culture, he learned about a negative and disturbing one as well.

The year was 1977, a time when the youth in the area were involved in vandalism, glue sniffing, and petty theft. To help raise the plummeting adult opinion of the kids in the area, George met with a friend for coffee to discuss ways to transform young people's energy from destructive to productive.

"I had a friendship with the Jesuit priest at St. Patrick's Church, Father Bob Scullin," says George. "We met in order to come up with a creative way to deal with the problem. At that time, adults were really down on kids.

"Our thought was to have young people do theater so that adults could experience them in a positive way. We came up with this wild idea of young people doing theater for adults instead of doing it for kids. So after wrangling eight hundred bucks from the city, we started a youth theater in the summer of 1978. The only thing we were missing was someone to run it."

Enter Stephanie Morrison.

As a 24-year-old woman with training in theater and dance, she was the ideal person to launch, direct, and grow the youth theater.

Now, having recently finished her 25th season as executive director of the Near West Theater, Stephanie is proud of the fact that in 2003 the theater was the only Cleveland arts group to win the Governor's Award in the new category of Community Development and Participation.

"We do five shows a year, and like to do musical theater because it involves the greatest number of people," says Stephanie. "We just auditioned 60-plus kids for *Jesus Christ Superstar.*"

Although the space they have used for their productions, originally an old Irish ballroom, has worked for them over the last two and a half decades, Stephanie is ready to move into a new space.

"We have to move," insists Stephanie. "We run two shows at a time right now, and we are on top of ourselves."

Managing a youth theater has its challenges, but when Stephanie and George reflect upon tough times in their marriage, what immediately comes to mind is parenthood.

"I remember struggling over who was going to assume what parenting responsibilities with our sons, Noah and Seth," says Stephanie. "We sought counseling for that, which is something I'm proud to admit."

"We needed someone to help us sort things out in a practical way," adds George.

Aside from gaining clarity on the day-to-day logistics of parenting, this couple felt counseling helped them appreciate each other more.

"I had lost touch with how to do that," admits Stephanie.

When this couple feels romance slipping away, they shift their focus from theater and from George's challenges at Lutheran Metropolitan Ministry to food. Whether eating at the Fulton Bar & Grill in Ohio City or Minh Anh Vietnamese Restaurant & Market at West 54th and Detroit, George and Stephanie have learned to reconnect by making conversation over a good meal.

With a 23-year age difference between them, this couple views their age gap as a minor disparity.

As their 21-year-old son Seth walks through the room during the interview, Stephanie asks for his input.

"Seth, would you like to comment on our differences?"

Seth maintains a neutral expression, looks at me, and instead states what he sees as a similarity between his parents.

"They're both weird."

"What if Tomorrow Doesn't Come?

CRYSTAL & STEVE DZURNAK

When you walk into Crystal and Steve Dzurnak's home, one thing becomes exceedingly clear. Family matters. Three of the four walls in their living room are covered with photographs of their four children, and a large picture of Crystal in her wedding gown takes center stage on the fourth wall, flanked by wedding photos of her and Steve.

Having been raised in a close-knit Greek Orthodox family, Crystal is accustomed to family traditions and family expectations.

"I come from a strict upbringing," explains Crystal. "My family is very Greek. The movie *My Big Fat Greek Wedding* is my life. My very first date in high school was my senior Christmas dance, and I had to have my younger sister be my chaperone."

Crystal remembers wanting to go to college and her father not wanting her to leave home. Because the father of one of her best friends allowed his daughter to go to Ashland College, Crystal's dad reluctantly gave Crystal permission to attend along with her.

"Little did my dad know I was going to get to college and meet this fine American man," says Crystal.

"For our first date, I took Crystal to a slaughterhouse," remembers Steve. "I had missed a field trip for one of my classes and had to make it up."

All the guys in Steve's class dared Crystal to go on the date, knowing that she would be in the company of blood-drained cows hanging by their feet. She took their dare and had a fabulous time with Steve.

(Steve leaves the room and returns with a memento from their first date, horns from one of the bulls that had been slaughtered.)

"We used to drink champagne and wine out of these horns," says Steve.

Crystal and Steve's courtship lasted for three years before they got married, but that first year was a difficult adjustment period for Crystal's family.

"When my family found out about me dating Steve, they tried to send me to Greece for the summer to be a camp counselor. My parents had no choice but to try to stop me from seeing Steve. It was their culture. Everybody in my family had married Greek. I was the very first not to," explains Crystal.

Steve and Crystal decided to get married, with or without Crystal's father's blessing. Eventually, Mr. Glynias did give them his blessing, and along with it, a wedding with 750 guests.

Now married 23 years, this couple has a formula for a strong marriage. Having stood their ground about getting married in the first place, Steve and Crystal have always made their marriage the number-one priority.

Having studied hotel and restaurant management in college, Steve worked at several Holiday Inns during the early years of their marriage, but because of the long and unpredictable hours, he decided to take a different position that would allow him to be home at the same time as Crystal.

"We never would have stayed married if Steve had kept working at hotels," says Crystal. "He worked all of the holidays and was often gone until three or four o'clock in the morning. He'd leave for work at two or three o'clock in the afternoon, when I was coming home from my job."

"I made a conscious decision to leave the hotel business. Sometimes you have to give up one thing for another," says Steve. "By no means do I regret making the decision to leave hotel management and go into sales."

A few years later, after all four of their children were born, this couple was faced with a situation that would once again give them the opportunity to decide to put their marriage first. At the time, they were living in a big house in Strongsville, and Steve was working two jobs while Crystal stayed home with the children.

Although Steve was under more stress than usual, he was surprised when he got on the scale one day and found he had lost 50 pounds in a month. Soon after, Steve began to have pains in his chest, leading Crystal to rush him to the emergency room. After a series of tests, doctors ruled out a heart attack and broke the news to Crystal and Steve, who was 27 at the time, that he had a cancerous mass in his chest.

"Before the diagnosis, when Steve was first sick, we decided to move into a smaller house," remembers Crystal.

"After I got sick, we asked ourselves how important our big house was to us and realized no house was worth the stress of working two jobs," explains Steve, "so we moved to a bungalow in Fairview Park."

Moving from their three-bathroom home to a one-bathroom bungalow was a huge adjustment for Crystal, Steve, and their four kids, but they put their relationship first and made the move.

Although scaling down their lifestyle was stressful, it was a walk in the park compared to the four months of chemotherapy and radiation treatments Steve had to endure. To make matters worse, the cancer returned one year later.

After Steve's second diagnosis, he seriously considered forgoing cancer therapy because he didn't want his wife and children to witness the suffering he had experienced during the first round of cancer treatment.

Crystal remembers convincing Steve to reconsider. "I made him come in the house and sit at the table. I looked at him and said, 'If you don't want to go through treatment again that is absolutely your choice, but before you decide, I want you to write a letter to each of your four kids and tell them why you can't be at their high school graduation.' He looked at me and said, 'That is so unfair.' I said, 'No, you not going through this treatment is what's unfair.' We held each other and cried."

When asked what commitment means to him in the context of marriage, Steve didn't have to think twice.

"Just picture the bottom falling out of your life. Imagine you've lost your job, you've gotten sick, you've gotten in an accident, and someone is suing you. Picture everything going wrong. Is that person going to be there with you or are they going to want to bail out? If that person will be there for you, that's commitment."

Steve speaks from experience. Crystal has been by his side not only through illness, but through financially sparse times as well. He claims it's her positive attitude that has made the difference in their marriage.

"Crystal is the more optimistic one between us," says Steve. "Anytime that I think we won't have enough money, she keeps me sane."

"We do what we have to do to survive," claims Crystal. "We're taking our very first vacation alone in years. We leave next week for a luxurious cabin in Tennessee. When I told Steve about it, he said we wouldn't be able to afford it. He worries about the finances and says things like 'What if this, what if that.' I tell him, 'What if tomorrow doesn't come?'"

Steve looks at Crystal and remembers. He has been much too close to knowing the answer to that question.

When I Fall in Love, It Will Be Forever

MARVIN & PEGGY MCMICKLE

As a seven-year-old child, Marvin McMickle had no idea that the man who came to dinner one evening in his home in Chicago was not only a music legend, but also the author of song lyrics that Marvin would one day recite to his wife, Peggy.

"Ever since the day Nat King Cole came to our house for dinner, I've been a great fan of his," says Marvin. "He had come to perform for the Elks Lodge in Chicago and stopped at our house to eat the chitlins my mother had made."

The Nat King Cole lyrics that Marvin recited to Peggy during their courtship became the theme for their wedding.

"In our wedding album, the photographer superimposed a photo of us over the sheet music, the lyrics of which read, 'When I fall in love, it will be forever. Or I'll never fall in love.'"

When Marvin first heard about Peggy from the dean of the school he was attending, Union Theological Seminary in New York City, falling in love was the furthest thought from his mind. Frankly, so was dating.

"When Dr. Lawrence Jones first told me about meeting Peggy, I didn't think much of it," says Marvin. "It was one of those situations where if she were to ever come to town, I might get together with her."

"I met Dr. Jones when I heard him speak at a church retreat that I had attended in Washington, D.C.," remembers Peggy. "I had agreed to be a hostess for the retreat because I thought it might be a good way for me to meet a nice young man."

Peggy fulfilled her obligation as hostess, and although she did not meet a young man at the retreat, she met someone who would lead her to the man of her dreams.

"Dr. Jones was the keynote speaker that day and talked about how people cope through crises," Peggy recalls. "He referred to the crises elderly people endure when they outlive their family and friends. Then he mentioned that young people deal with crises as well, especially when they can't find the right companion or right relationship."

Peggy heard Dr. Jones's compassion for a young person's dilemma and felt he was speaking directly to her. After his speech, she approached him and asked a question that changed her life forever: "By the way, do you know any nice young men?"

Admitting that he knew several eligible bachelors, Dr. Jones gave Peggy his number at Union Theological Seminary and suggested she call him if she were to ever visit New York City.

Six months later, Peggy retrieved the raggedy piece of paper on which she had written Dr. Jones's phone number and followed through on his suggestion to call him.

"It was Valentine's Day weekend when I was in New York City on vacation with friends doing a theater tour," explains Peggy. "When I called Dr. Jones, he said he knew of a nice young man who would give me a call at my hotel and take me to dinner."

"When Dr. Jones called me and asked me to take Peggy to dinner, I told him that I didn't go on blind dates," says Marvin. "Then I remembered that he was in charge of financial aid. I agreed to do it."

When Marvin called the hotel Peggy was staying at in New York City, the hotel clerk told him there was no one registered at the hotel by the name of Peggy Noble. Marvin hung up the phone and was about to let his single effort be enough until he remembered the influence Dr. Jones had on financial aid.

He called again.

When the clerk said, "I told you, there is no one here by the name of Peggy Noble," Marvin hung up the phone, got in his car, and drove to the hotel.

Marvin chuckles and says, "Financial aid makes you do strange things."

Once at the hotel, Marvin asked the clerk, face to face this time, about whether or not Peggy Noble was registered there. The clerk said, "Sir, I told you that she is not registered in this hotel. But if you want to look at the registry for yourself, go ahead."

Marvin took the registry from the hotel clerk and scanned the names on the list. Had he not looked on the very last page, he would have missed seeing that Peggy Noble was, indeed, registered at the hotel.

After a significant amount of time had elapsed, Peggy assumed Marvin was not going to call her, so she accepted an invitation to go on a sightseeing tour with her friends.

"I was in the hallway waiting for the elevator when I heard the phone ring in my room," remembers Peggy. "Thinking the call might be from Marvin, I ran to open my door, jumped over the bed, and answered the phone. It was Marvin."

Peggy and Marvin's dinner date lasted three hours that night, and Cupid didn't leave the table until his job was complete.

"During the three hours at dinner, we fell in love," says Peggy. "I remember thinking that Marvin was the person I'd been waiting for."

Although Peggy and Marvin found one another interesting, they agree that each of them fell in love with the other's spirit, rather than their physical appearance or ability to make conversation.

"After I returned to Washington, D.C., Marvin called me and said, 'You know, I can't even remember your features, but I think I'm in love with you.' I told him that I felt the same way. I couldn't remember his face, but his spirit had stayed with me."

When Dr. Jones learned of Marvin and Peggy's already intense relationship, he advised Marvin to slow down. Financial aid or no financial aid, this time Marvin rejected Dr. Jones's advice.

"We were engaged in less than a month of meeting each other and were married in less than four months, on June 7, 1975," recalls Marvin. "When you know it's right, you know it's right."

When this Shaker Heights couple reflects on how they were brought together, they're convinced the meeting was meant to be.

"I do feel our meeting one another was predestined," asserts Marvin, "in the sense that all of the circumstances of our meeting could not have come together randomly. I don't think I would have been ready to date Peggy had it been six months earlier."

"Because of the fact that I almost turned down the opportunity to attend the church retreat, that the hotel clerk told Marvin I wasn't recorded as being registered, and that I almost wasn't in the room when he called, there were so many chances for us to miss each other," explains Peggy.

A year after they were married, Marvin was called to St. Paul's Baptist Church in Montclair, New Jersey. While they were on the East Coast, Peggy worked for the federal government in public health, and gave birth to their son, Aaron.

In its computer search for a minister in 1987, Antioch Baptist Church in Cleveland came across the name and profile of Reverend Marvin McMickle. When the search committee invited Marvin to Cleveland for an interview, he was less than enthused.

"At the time I was invited to visit Antioch Baptist Church, nothing about coming to Cleveland appealed to me," admits Marvin, "but Peggy persuaded me to talk to the search committee. I have to say that I was very favorably impressed with the city, the church, and the people, as was Peggy when she visited Cleveland the next time I came to town."

After 28 years of marriage and 30 years as a pastor who does premarital and postmarital counseling, Marvin has strong ideas on what makes a marriage work, which he expresses in his book *Before We Say I Do: 7 Steps to a Healthy Marriage* (Judson Press, 2003).

"I wanted to create a tool based on my observation of the experiences of couples that could help me help them be successful in marriage," explains Marvin. "The thesis of the book is that success in marriage is based on what you do before you say 'I do.' Premarital counseling makes the need for postmarital counseling substantially less."

So strongly does Marvin feel about the importance of premarital counseling that a couple may not be married in Antioch Baptist Church unless the partners are willing to go through the process.

When asked if he and Peggy went through premarital counseling before getting married, they claim that they did.

"We discussed virtually everything that is in my book before we got married," says Marvin. "In essence, we developed our own premarital survey."

Inventories, surveys, and tests aside, Peggy McMickle needs no score or indicator for what she has always known. "It's a special joy to find your soulmate, the one person you want to be with. For me, that person is Marvin."

A Bull's-Eye for Cupid

WILMA SMITH & TOM GERBER

"Oh, God, don't let me run out of leg" was Tom Gerber's first thought as he stood up to meet Wilma Smith.

"Aside from being aware that she was tall," says Tom, "I was struck by the fact that Wilma was even better looking in person than she was on television."

When Wilma watched Tom stand as she entered Stouffer's Top of the Town restaurant in 1980, she was impressed by his chivalry.

"When Tom got up from his chair, I thought, *What a gentleman,*" remembers Wilma. "Unfortunately, men don't do the finer things anymore, and they really should."

Tom and Wilma's introduction to one another was a year in the making. The man who played cupid was Tom's next-door neighbor, Gary Ritchie, who was the news director at WEWS Channel 5 at the time.

"I had gone through a divorce," says Tom, "and Gary kept telling me about a woman he wanted me to meet who was an on-air personality and was also divorced. I told him I didn't want to have anything to do with someone who was an on-air personality, but he wouldn't stop trying to convince me to meet her. After about a year, I finally agreed to meet this woman under the condition that we would all go to lunch together. I made him promise me that if I went to lunch, he would stop bugging me about it."

While the news director of Channel 5 was working on Tom to meet Wilma, he was also trying to persuade Wilma to meet Tom.

"Gary kept telling me that he had a man he wanted me to meet," says Wilma. "I told him I didn't want to be fixed up and explained that it could be embarrassing if we didn't like each other or didn't know what to talk about."

That day, on the way to lunch with Wilma, Gary informed her that the man he had been telling her about was going to join them at the restaurant, but was only going to stay for coffee.

"Tom stayed for an hour and a half," says Wilma. "Little did I know that he had been invited for lunch rather than just coffee."

During their time at the restaurant, Wilma learned that Tom owned Brookside Meats, a family business that had been started by Tom's grandfather. When Wilma told him how her parents had always remarked about the high quality of Brookside's lunchmeat, Tom offered to send Wilma a care package of assorted products to give to her parents.

"When I received the package, I sent Tom a thank-you note and invited him to come and get a tour of the station," recalls Wilma.

That station tour kicked off a courtship that lasted nine months. During that time, Wilma and Tom spent many evenings eating dinner together between Wilma's news broadcasts at Channel 5. The more time Wilma spent with Tom, the more she began to care for him.

"Aside from my dad, Tom is truly the nicest man I have ever known," says Wilma. "He has an inner goodness about him and a very kind heart. He's someone I'm so proud to know, let alone be loved by."

With pride and love in her heart, Wilma acted impulsively the following Christmas Eve and called Tom at four o'clock in the morning to ask him a question he wasn't expecting.

"We had planned on getting married," explains Wilma, "but my father had been sick with a heart problem, and I was worried about my parents not being able to attend the wedding. I wanted to marry Tom and make sure I didn't lose him, so I called him early on Christmas Eve morning and said, 'Hi! What are you doing today?' He told me he had some deliveries to make, but that he could see me in the afternoon. Then I said, 'Do you think maybe we could get married today?' All I heard was silence."

"At that moment, my life flashed before my eyes," kids Tom. "I knew if I said 'No,' she'd be gone. If I said, 'yes,' then I'd have to get married. I said, 'yes,' but because it was Christmas Eve, I didn't think she could pull it off. At that point in our relationship, I learned that if you give Wilma a task, she gets it done."

As soon as business hours began on Christmas Eve, Wilma launched a search for a judge to marry them that afternoon. After a few phone calls, she found one who was willing to perform their wedding ceremony that afternoon in the library of his Bratenahl home.

"At ten o'clock that same morning, I called Tom back and told him we were getting married," says Wilma. "Tom was spending the day with his three sons. I remember when I got in the car and the boys asked their dad what we were doing for the day, he told them we were getting married. When I turned around to look at them, their eyes were as big as 50-cent pieces. We drove off and eloped."

After 23 years of marriage, Wilma and Tom agree that one of the reasons their marriage works so well is because of their different temperaments.

"I'm a worrier," admits Wilma. "I have been since I was a child. Sometimes I worry to the point that I can't sleep."

"I'm much more easygoing," says Tom. "If I were getting executed tomorrow, I'd sleep perfectly tonight."

This couple's opposite reactions to stressful situations helped them get through one of the hardest times in their marriage. After Wilma's dad passed away, her mom came to live with her and Tom for a three-year period.

"Although I am so grateful for the time I had with my mom while she lived with us, it was not always easy," says Wilma. "When people are ill, they're often not themselves. A situation like that can put a strain on a relationship. Our home is our haven, but at times the strain would take away from that haven. Even though it was a stressful situation, Tom understood how important it was for me to have that special time with my mom. He was incredibly supportive, something for which I have always respected him."

As a news anchor for Fox 8 News, Wilma's life is often dictated by a full schedule of activities. As a project manager for Forest City Enterprises, Tom's schedule is no less hectic. When together, what they love to do most is to simply be at home.

"I'm a real nester," says Wilma. "When I'm home with our three beagles and Tom, I'm happy."

For Tom, splitting wood to burn in their fireplaces or getting on the tractor and cutting the lawn is what feeds his soul.

Whether relaxing by a fire or playing with their beagles, Wilma and Tom will forever be grateful to their friend, Gary Ritchie.

"He was a very persistent cupid," says Wilma.

Lucky for them.

They Will Survive

CLARA & ALEX HERTZ

Go to Severance Athletic Club in Cleveland Heights Monday through Friday and you'll see them walking the track, hand in hand. Both 81 years old and Holocaust survivors, Clara and Alex Hertz are committed to the idea of living life to the fullest. For them, one way to do so is to keep moving.

"We've been exercising for 30 years," says Clara. "We were exercising when exercising wasn't fashionable."

Although Clara has lost much of her eyesight and Alex recently underwent a thyroid operation, they haven't let those obstacles interfere with their daily discipline of walking together.

This couple's longevity and zest for life are in part due to a skill they were forced to learn at a young age—the skill of survival. Clara and Alex not only appreciate every day they wake up, they appreciate every day they wake up next to each other.

Born in 1922 in a small village in Hungary, Alex Hertz lived with his parents and one brother. One day in 1942, a group of Hungarian men stole him away from his family and took him to a labor camp where he worked in a steel factory.

"We couldn't go into the army because we were Jewish," says Alex. "So we were sent to labor camps."

After two years in a labor camp, Alex and many others were taken to Austria by train. While there, they spent six months dig-

133

ging trenches for the Germans, in preparation for the continued war. From there they were taken to another camp in Austria for one month, and then to another camp in Germany.

"I remember walking from the camp in Austria to the camp in Germany," says Alex. "It was winter, and we were picking up dead people and putting them into holes that had been dug. We, ourselves, were given only enough food so not to die."

During Alex's time in the labor camps, his parents were taken to Auschwitz. He never saw them again.

The exact same year that Alex was wrenched away from his parents, Clara was separated from her mother, father, and four brothers.

"We lived in a small town in Hungary and had a very nice life," says Clara. "We weren't rich, but we were comfortable. I had very good memories as a child. We never felt any anti-Semitism in our village until the Germans came in. One day we were fine, and the next day the Germans show up. We had heard about Hitler invading Poland, but we had no idea he was coming to Hungary."

Clara will never forget the day the Germans came to her grandfather's farm and made him sign over his property. One man, in particular, would visit Clara's family's grocery store over the course of several weeks. Afraid that the man was beginning to like her, Clara would try not to be home whenever he'd stop by.

"The night before they took us away, that man came to our house while we were having dinner," remembers Clara. "He told me he wanted to talk to me. I told him that whatever he had to say, he would have to say in front of my family. He told me the Germans were coming the following day to take us away. He said he wanted me to go with him so that he could save me. I remember telling him that I didn't know where they were going to take us, but that I wasn't going to leave my family."

The following day, Clara's family, along with many other Jewish families, was taken from their home and herded into a big schoolyard. After two days in the schoolyard, they were taken to another town where they boarded a train to Auschwitz.

"They put us in a cattle car with no air and nothing to eat," remembers Clara. "We couldn't move. Some of the people went crazy. Some of them died. When they finally opened the door for us to get out, I could smell burning flesh. It was a horrible smell. I was so confused. Suddenly, they divided us. I was separated from my mother, my father, and my brothers. They took me away, and I never saw any of my family again."

While in Auschwitz for two weeks, Clara endured a ritual that was degrading and terrifying. Every day at four o'clock in the morning, the Germans would make people line up in front of them stark naked. If they didn't like how the inmates looked, the soldiers would put them in a wagon and take them to a room where they would be gassed and dropped into a crematorium.

"It was terrifying," says Clara. "You never knew when your time was coming."

Because the Germans needed men, women, and children to work for them in factories, they put hundreds of people back on a train and sent them to a city in Germany. Clara was on that train.

"I worked in a textile factory making clothes for soldiers," explains Clara. "They made us wear a gray-and-blue striped prison uniform. We were allowed to take a shower, but we had to wear the same uniform each day. They fed us only enough to keep us alive, usually a piece of bread and some soup every 12 hours."

In December of 1944, the Germans ordered Clara and the group she was with to leave the textile factory. After each of them received a piece of bread, they were forced to walk to a labor camp. From December through March, Clara, along with hundreds of other people, walked through several towns and over two mountains. Many died along the way.

"When I got back to camp, there were piles of dead people, four feet high," says Clara. "Those of us who were still alive were put into a small room together, shoulder to shoulder. Lice were eating our skin and our scalp. I saw friends I grew up with die next to me."

Although Clara got typhus and her weight dropped to only 45 pounds, she was determined to stay alive.

"One day a German doctor came into my room and said, 'Tomorrow, you're going to die,'" recalls Clara. "I looked at him and said, 'Damn you. I'm not going to die.'

"I made myself to live. I didn't want my parents finding me in a pile of dead people."

In 1945, the British liberated everyone in the camp and sent them to Sweden to recuperate. When Clara gained her strength, she wrote to her mother's family in the United States. After Clara's uncle received her letter, he sent her the proper paperwork and a ticket for her voyage to America.

"When I got to the United States, I thought I was going crazy," remembers Clara. "I knew I had lost my family. I couldn't sleep, so I'd walk the streets. At that time, there were no psychologists or psychiatrists to talk to. All I had was myself. I realized I had to go on."

Three years after Clara settled in Cleveland, Alex arrived in the United States. He, too, had an uncle who had sent him the paperwork to bring him to America.

Although Clara lived in Cleveland and Alex lived in New York, destiny took a hand in bringing them together.

"My cousins took me to their parents' house in New York, and that is where I met Alex," explains Clara. "My aunt and uncle knew Alex's aunt and uncle and invited them and Alex to their house."

The attraction between Clara and Alex was sparked on a rainy summer day. Running from the rain, they took refuge under a cabana. It was there that Alex first kissed Clara.

Alex remembers his wife's stunning features. "She was a nice-looking girl with a full head of black hair and beautiful high cheekbones."

"The first time I saw Alex, I knew I wanted to know this guy better," says Clara. "He was so gorgeous with his beautiful blond hair and big shoulders."

Admittedly, Alex and Clara were physically attracted to one another at first sight, but it was more than sexual chemistry that led them to get married and stay married for 53 years.

"We've been partners," says Clara. "I'm outgoing and he's quiet, so what I can't do, Alex can do, and what he can't do, I can do. When Alex started his carpentry business, I stayed home to raise our three children and help him with his work by answering phones and taking messages."

This couple's marital longevity can be credited to their complementary personalities, no doubt, but it was their common Holocaust experience 60 years ago that has made them kindred spirits. Having both lost their families, become prisoners, and faced death straight on, they recognize in each other a quality that has made them strong as individuals, and even stronger as a couple—the indefatigable will to live.

With Five You Get Family

MARY & MARK JOHNSON

While interviewing Mary and Mark Johnson on one of the sets in the Channel 5 television studios, I sit back and watch them volley compliments back and forth. I listen to each of them claim that the other is the stronger of the two, and finally make my own decision. It's a toss-up.

"Mark has a faith that astonishes people when they get to know him," says Mary. "He's got this wonderful belief in God that I wish I had 25 percent of."

"Mary has more strength and bravery in her little pinky than I'll ever have," insists Mark.

Mary turns to face Mark. "I don't understand it when you say I'm strong."

"She's a rock in an emergency," continues Mark. "She has so much wit, smarts, and sense of what to do to solve a problem."

"I don't see it as strength," says Mary. "I just do it."

Mary used her "just do it" attitude while raising her three children during her first husband's five-year battle with cancer, which, sadly, he lost.

"During the last 90 days of my husband's life, I made the drive from Ashtabula to Euclid and back every day because I had to," explains Mary. "When you have to do something, you will do it."

"When you hear Mary's story, you understand how strong she

really is," says Mark. "At one point, she had three kids, her husband was dying of cancer, he had to leave his job, they couldn't pay the bills, the house was auctioned off for sale, and Mary had to work three jobs to survive."

Mark learned of Mary's personal hardships from her 14-year-old twin sons, whom he was mentoring while directing a youth group at St. Joseph's Church in Ashtabula County.

"One day Mary's sons, Mike and Ray, invited me to hang out with them at their house, and that's when I met their mom and 10-year-old sister, Lisa," recalls Mark. "Before I started dating Mary, we did things as a fivesome. The kids and Mary would come visit me in Akron, where I was working as a weather forecaster at a television station."

Mary chuckles. "It gave a whole new definition to group dating."

As time passed, Mark and Mary talked a lot on the phone and became very close friends. It didn't take long, however, before they realized they were feeling more than friendly toward one another.

"Mary started out as my relationship coach and would encourage me to date different women, but that didn't last very long," says Mark. "One day I realized that I really enjoyed spending time with her. Whenever I'd be on a date with another woman, I'd find myself thinking about the next time I would be with Mary and the kids."

A year and two months later, Mark decided he wanted to be with Mary and her children for the rest of his life. When he proposed, he not only did it in a romantic setting, but with thousands of people watching.

"There was no way I could turn down Mark's proposal in front of everyone in Cleveland," says Mary.

"I proposed to her on the Love Boat during *The Morning Exchange*," explains Mark. "We were airing that week's show live on an Alaskan cruise ship. While on the cruise, Mary would wake up early each morning and help set up the equipment for the show. The morning of the proposal, I knocked on her cabin door and asked her to help as usual. That morning, she told me she wanted to sleep."

"I really didn't want to wake up," recalls Mary. "Mark kept asking me until I said, 'Okay, fine. I'll help, but I'm not doing my hair or putting on makeup.'"

With windblown hair and minus makeup, Mary was stunned when at one point during the live broadcast, Mark pulled her in front of the television camera and said, "Honey, would you marry me?"

Mary looked into the camera and said, "I'll get him for this," but then turned to Mark and said, "Yes."

Mark knew that in order for them to truly be a family, Mary's kids would have to accept him, so he proposed to them as well. He gathered them together and explained that he had asked their mom to marry him. He told Mary's children he knew he could never replace their father and that he would never try to, but if they would let him, he could be a dad to them. In lieu of an engagement ring, Mark gave each of Mary's children a gold watch.

On December 30, 1994, 275 people attended Mark and Mary's wedding.

"We have two of the largest families in Ashtabula County, so we limited it to first cousins and up," says Mark. "At the reception, we had the world's largest chicken dance circle I've ever seen."

Now married eight years, this couple has faced some challenging situations. Within the first two years of matrimony, they sent two kids off to college, lost Mary's mother unexpectedly, and were told that Mary had uterine cancer.

"The 'C word' is the scariest word you can ever hear," says Mark. "The blessing was that Mary's cancer was a bleeding cancer and was caught early. Uterine cancer often grows without much fanfare. Usually, you don't catch it until it metastasizes, but because of the bleeding, the doctors caught it in stage 1."

"In February, I had a normal Pap smear," says Mary. "When I started bleeding, I knew it wasn't blood from my period. I knew it wasn't normal. I went to the doctor at the end of May, and on

June 10th had surgery. I'm a firm advocate of knowing my body and having physicals. Knowing my body and what was wrong for me is what saved my life."

Mark and Mary Johnson are realists. Understanding that challenges are a part of life, they are candid about day-to-day struggles.

"Mary's Slovak and I'm Irish, so when we argue it's loud and fun," says Mark. "But then we kiss and make up."

"When we had marriage counseling in our church before we got married, we were told to never let the sun go down upon our wrath," explains Mary. "Well, some nights in the Johnson household, the sun doesn't set."

Mark admits that one of the hardest lessons he has had to learn has been to not fix all of Mary's problems. There was a time when Mary would come home and vent about her day, and Mark would always try to give her advice.

Mark's experience as a weather forecaster has helped him gain perspective on the situation. "Sometimes it wasn't until after an argument that I'd realize Mary was just giving me a weather report," says Mark. "She was just giving me information and didn't want me to solve the problem. She just wanted me to listen."

Over the years, Mark has wondered how their children have viewed their disagreements,

"At times we spat when the kids are around," says Mark. "But when they see us resolving problems, they feel safe and secure."

On the other side of the coin, Mark and Mary do not hide the love and affection they have for each other.

"Our kids have seen how much we love each other," says Mark. "For example, when we shower together, we tell them we're going up to take a shower. The kids are all 20-something now, so they're old enough to know we love each other in an intimate way."

Whether this couple is quarreling into the wee hours of the night or kissing and making up in the shower, they agree on the bottom line.

"You can't plan life," says Mary. "You just have to love each other."

"The foundation must be strong," explains Mark. "Because if the foundation is strong, any storm that blows the roof off isn't going to take the house down."

Coming from a meteorologist, that's good advice.

She's an ENFJ, He's an ENTJ

BOBBI & ROY CHURCH

Neither of them cared much for the idea of a blind date. Both undergraduate students at the State University of New York at Cortland in the 1960s, Roy and Bobbi were talked into going out with each other, Roy by his roommate and Bobbi by her sorority sister.

"I remember exactly what I wore," says Bobbi. "I really didn't want to go on this date, so I just threw on a blue A-line skirt and a little sweater. I didn't prepare or primp at all for the evening."

Although their first date turned out to be a pleasant night at the movies, it wasn't until their second date that indelible impressions were made.

"I'll always remember how caring Roy was on our second date," says Bobbi. "We went sledding, and because I had worn a windbreaker, I was freezing. He gave me his jacket to wear. That really impressed me."

Roy's initial take on Bobbi wasn't quite so positive. Although he found her to be very cute, interesting, and easy to talk to, he felt extremely intimidated.

"I took one look at her and thought she was way out of my league," recalls Roy. "She was so well dressed and obviously part of the Long Island scene, where she had grown up. I was a farm boy from a relatively poor farm in upstate New York."

Despite Roy's discomfort, he continued to date Bobbi when she returned to campus after a few months of student teaching. The following summer Roy's angst about their opposing backgrounds returned when Bobbi invited him to visit her on suburban Long Island.

"I was out of place on Long Island," says Roy. "I had driven to see Bobbi in my father's old Nash Rambler. I didn't realize how much it would cost to pay tolls. What little cash I brought was soon gone. I was so out of it. I didn't even dress right."

To make matters even more strained, Bobbi was feeling confused during Roy's visit. She had had a high school sweetheart for whom she still had strong feelings, and she wasn't exactly sure where her heart belonged.

"I was so impressed with how Roy dealt with my state of turmoil," says Bobbi. "He didn't get mad. I'll always remember what he said. He said, 'I'm not going to pick up all my marbles and go home.' He wanted to let time take over to see how our relationship would go."

With a sense of faith in his heart and a $20 bill in his pocket that Bobbi's father had slipped him as he left, Roy drove back home. As he pulled into his father's driveway with only a quarter left in his pocket, Roy appreciated Bobbi's father's generous gesture and knew that although his economic status was strikingly different from Bobbi's, her family was gracious, loving, and accepting of him.

Bobbi returned to campus that next fall as a senior and saw Roy, who was a junior and in training for the upcoming football season. At that point, she decided that even if Roy had wanted to "pick up all his marbles," she wasn't going to let him go home with them. Although Roy had invited another girl to the homecoming dance, Bobbi, with the help of her sorority sisters, dressed herself up and went to the party with the sole intention of letting Roy know that her boyfriend confusion had waned. She knew which young man she wanted, and that young man was Roy.

After homecoming, there was no doubt in Roy's mind as to how Bobbi felt about him. The feelings were mutual. They were in love and felt it was time for Bobbi to visit the farm and meet Roy's family.

"I thought I knew about farms," says Bobbi. "You know, cows, hay, and all that."

It wasn't until Roy brought her home to meet his family that Bobbi realized life on the farm was diametrically opposed to life on Long Island.

"I remember standing at the front door of Roy's house dressed in my little matching slacks, top, and hair bow. I was so nervous. Once I crossed the threshold, I could sense a distinct difference between my upbringing and his. Life on the farm was much more informal and relaxed than I was used to."

"We were very aware of the fact that we had come from completely different backgrounds," explains Roy. "Luckily we were both processors and spent a lot of time talking about how we could be in a relationship without being in conflict."

Back in the 1960s, when couples often married because it was what most people did in their early twenties, this couple was ahead of their time. Instead of focusing only on the details of their wedding, Roy and Bobbi devoted most of their time to talking about the possible pitfalls of marriage, with the intention of learning the most they could about each other's values, financial habits, and lifelong goals.

"Each of us valued education and felt there was worth in helping people," says Bobbi.

"We both wanted to be in a setting that would be intellectually challenging," adds Roy. "Part of that is a bias I brought to the relationship, having grown up with the bovines. A lot of my working hours were spent doing repetitive, mundane activities on the farm. Because of that, I wanted to spend the rest of my life in an environment where I could have a chance to grow and develop."

Grow and develop is exactly what Roy and Bobbi did. After they moved to Florida, Bobbi pursued her teaching career as an elementary school teacher and earned a master's degree in reading. Roy began his career as a college instructor and steadily moved up the academic ladder, enjoying a variety of administrative positions that eventually brought him to Cleveland, where he thrives today as the president of Lorain County Community College.

Teaching and working in the academic world gave Roy and Bobbi the intellectual fulfillment they had been searching for—as well as exposure to the Meyers-Briggs Type Indicator, a personality test that confirmed for them why they were meant for each other.

"That test was an eye-opener," says Bobbi. "I was running a reading lab at a school in Florida, and the school sent the teachers up to the University of Florida in Gainesville to study their lab. Part of that training included taking the Meyers-Briggs. After I took it, it was an awakening. For the first time in my life, I understood why people looked at the world differently."

After Roy took the test, the results proved to him and Bobbi what they had suspected all along. They looked at life almost identically.

Bobbi's results showed her to be an ENFJ, and Roy's test showed him to be an ENTJ. Each letter of the test score represents a part of your personality. In Bobbi and Roy's case the *N* in both of their scores meant they were both "intuitors." Translated into everyday language, their test results meant that they loved to process thoughts and ideas. While another couple might spend minutes making a major decision, Roy and Bobbi most likely take hours or even days to talk about the meaning and value of their choices before making a life-altering decision.

Their "processing" nature stood them in good stead when they had to deal with one of the biggest challenges in their marriage: infertility. After getting his doctorate degree, Roy began a new position at a different college in Florida at a time when he and Bobbi had spent years trying to get pregnant.

"That was a nightmare time in our marriage," remembers Bobbi. "I couldn't get pregnant. Roy was consumed with his new job. I was alone living in a new community, working at a job I didn't like. I suffered from severe depression at a time when we didn't know about Prozac."

This traumatic juncture in their lives was just one more reason for Bobbi and Roy to do what they loved doing most. Discuss, discuss, discuss. Their ability to process and talk about their values and dreams is what led them to decide to adopt their son and daughter.

Roy admits that it would be easy to allow his job to consume his life, but he works diligently at balancing the time he spends on the job with the time he spends with Bobbi and his children.

He explains that he used to be an ENTJ but is becoming more of an INTJ. The *E* stands for extrovert, and the *I* stands for introvert.

"I've become more of an introvert over the years," says Roy. "I'm such an extrovert in my job that I find myself wanting to retreat into our relationship when I get home. Our home is a wonderful haven for me."

This Avon Lake couple agrees. The time they put into discussing their future together before they got married paved the way for them to continue talking after they were married, and the test results are in. Their score? Thirty-five years of a strong, successful marriage.

Returning from a
World of Hurt

DOUG POWELL &
MARY REYNOLDS POWELL

Doug and Mary Powell have a lot in common. They were raised less than 20 miles apart in large Catholic families in New York State, and both were educated in medicine. It was the time they spent together in Vietnam, however, that created the ties that have bound them for a lifetime.

As a nurse in Vietnam from November of 1970 to November of 1971, Mary was stationed at the 24th Evacuation Hospital at Long Binh. While there, she treated soldiers suffering from a variety of tropical diseases.

"I took care of guys who were not blown apart in the war, but who were being brought in from the jungle and were suffering from malaria, typhus, dengue fever, and encephalitis. It wasn't unusual for someone to be six feet, two inches tall and weigh 130 pounds. In order for these men to be evacuated from the bush for medical reasons, their fevers had to reach 104 degrees."

The night Mary met Doug, she encountered two things she had never seen before on her ward: a very sick one-month-old Vietnamese infant in a crib and an army pediatrician dressed in street clothes. That pediatrician was Doug.

"I remember watching Doug come through the back door of the ward," says Mary. "What made him immediately stand out was that he wasn't in uniform. He was in bell-bottom pants and a denim shirt. That was a big shock because most of the doctors hung around in their fatigues. It was as if Doug had walked in from 'the world.' When he came over to me, he started visiting and was so easy to talk to."

By the time Mary met Doug, she had been in Vietnam for four months. The previous pediatrician didn't understand why nurses would be interested in the details of a patient's condition or the history of a disease. One of the things that impressed Mary most about Doug was his willingness to engage in medical conversation and answer all of her questions.

"Mary was great at starting IVs on the soldiers, but because she wasn't used to treating infants, she didn't want to restart the scalp IV that had slipped out of this baby who had been admitted earlier that day with neonatal hepatitis," recalls Doug. "I was quite impressed with Mary. She stood there in her nurse's uniform, green fatigues, and combat boots. She was quite cute and so delightfully easy to talk to."

Two weeks later, when Doug asked Mary to dinner, she accepted his invitation but suggested they go to the officers' club for the monthly "Cook Your Own Steak" party.

"The officers' club was nothing like what we think of as a club," explains Mary. "Although it had a long bar with bar stools, it was a brown wooden room built on a concrete slab. Parachute material was suspended over a concrete patio to keep out the rain."

Doug was a little uptight on their first date because Mary knew all of the doctors at the dinner party and he didn't. Being the new kid on the block, he hadn't met very many people. By the time he and Mary went back to her hooch, his nervousness had subsided, and they talked until four o'clock in the morning.

During one of their conversations that night, Mary asked Doug if he had a family. Doug told Mary he had a mother, father, and brothers, but the response Mary was looking for had to do with marital status rather than family of origin.

"A lot of the men were 'geographical bachelors,'" explains Mary. "Until I met Doug, I was bitter and very distrustful of men, as well as being bitter about the war."

During the seven months they spent together in Vietnam, Doug and Mary's relationship went through several different stages. They had fun at first, but over time, Mary felt Doug was getting a little too close to her emotionally. Mary began to pull away from Doug, but he was patient and waited for her to work through her feelings.

"By Doug hanging in there, it affirmed something in me that had been buried," says Mary. "I hadn't been able to trust men for so long. Doug helped me see that I could have a caring relationship."

Before returning to the United States, Doug and Mary traveled together throughout Asia and Australia. Once they returned to the United States, they weren't completely sure how their relationship would hold up in the "real world," especially after they had served in such a controversial war.

"Coming back from Vietnam, everything was abnormal," says Mary. "I wasn't safe in conversations for a good six months. My disorientation was all related to anger about what the United States was doing in Vietnam. By the time we returned home, nobody cared about what was happening on the other side of the earth. At that point, even antiwar demonstrators had stopped demonstrating."

Once back in America, Mary found herself to be very sensitive to conflict. "I remember being at my brother's hockey game and watching people cheering after a fight broke out. I just sat there and sobbed. Violence is always the same whether it's in a war or on the ice."

Although Mary had finished serving her time in the army, Doug had five months left to serve, and did so at Fort Carson in Colorado Springs. Mary decided to follow Doug out west and take a job in Denver.

"When Doug moved from Colorado Springs to Denver, we had to redefine our relationship again," explains Mary. "We were leading two separate lives and couldn't seem to make the gears mesh. We split up for a while."

After a monthlong break-up, they realized they not only wanted to reunite, they wanted to be married.

After getting married in Denver in July of 1973, Mary and Doug pursued their medical careers. Following a three-month struggle with hospital bureaucracy and a stint in public health nursing, Mary decided to go to graduate school for a master's degree in urban sociology, which paved the way for the many years she has spent working on community health issues such as domestic violence and Alzheimer's disease.

While Mary was earning her master's degree, Doug was realizing he would rather take care of premature newborn babies as a neonatalogist than be a pediatrician. Doug's medical career took him, Mary, and their three children to Kalamazoo, Michigan, Albany, New York, and finally to Cleveland, where he currently works with newborn babies at Huron Hospital.

Mary and Doug both agree that Doug's schedule as a doctor has been the biggest challenge in their marriage.

"I think that initially I was totally wrapped up in my work," admits Doug. "It was a real ego thing. To be a doctor and save little babies was very ego-fulfilling."

"Three years into Doug's career, I told him that his schedule was insane," recalls Mary. "Adjusting to Doug's hours when the kids were little was extremely difficult. In Kalamazoo, Michigan, Doug worked in the hospital for 24 hours, was off 24 hours, was on 8 hours, and the next day on another 24 hours. Three times a year he had off Friday, Saturday, and Sunday.

"When Doug told me that his hours were a fact of life, I decided I would create a life for the kids and me, and when Doug entered it, he entered it. I was determined not to have any expectations. My whole makeup was based on a can-do attitude. I felt I could pull it off by being Superwoman."

Mary's staunch determination to get through Doug's horrendous work hours was instrumental in keeping their marriage together, but even she admits that the move to Albany saved their marriage.

"Doug was astounded when he heard me mention to someone one night that if we had stayed in Kalamazoo, we probably would have gotten divorced," remembers Mary. "The move to Albany was important, but we also truly loved each other. When we connected, we really connected."

Thirty-some years after being together in Vietnam, Mary and Doug do not claim to have seen the worst of the war. What Mary did see she put in a book she has written called *A World of Hurt— Between Innocence and Arrogance in Vietnam* (Greenleaf Enterprises, 2000).

"Neither of us was out getting shot at," says Doug. "We have complete sympathy for those Vietnam veterans who were actually in the hardcore war. But I think I would have difficulty relating long term with someone who hadn't seen what I had seen."

Mary feels the same way as Doug, and says so in these lines from the dedication of her book:

For Doug
who has always understood

Not Just Another
Church Meeting

JOYCE & TIM JAMES

In 1984, two years after her divorce, Joyce James went searching for a new church for herself and her four-year-old son. She found the church all right, but along with it she found something completely unexpected. She found a husband.

"I didn't go to church looking for a husband," insists Joyce. "I had been in a large congregation and was looking for a smaller church. I was prayerful and sincere in finding a church that my four-year-old son and I could get involved in."

So when Joyce's friend invited her to visit Fifth Christian Church in Cleveland, she decided to give it a try. Reverend Tim James noticed Joyce as a consistent visitor, but it wasn't until after 10 months that he approached her about joining the church.

"After Joyce became a member, I noticed other men becoming interested in her," remembers Tim. "I didn't want to come across as the big rooster in the chicken coop, so I decided to give the other men their chance."

Tim gave the other men about a year and then approached Joyce with an invitation to a Valentine's Day dinner dance sponsored by the women in the church.

"I had no idea Tim was interested in me," says Joyce. "When

he asked me to attend an activity for that evening, I thought we were going to a meeting of some kind. When we arrived at the dinner dance, we had to sit at the head table. I remember everyone looking at us and whispering."

After the church dinner, Tim and Joyce spent the rest of the evening dancing and laughing at a lounge at a nearby Holiday Inn. Although they had a wonderful time together, Tim called Joyce the next day and explained that he never dated any one person too often and that he thought they shouldn't get involved.

"I had gone through a divorce myself," says Tim. "I didn't want to get into a relationship until I knew I was clear about who I was. I needed time to prepare myself for the right person. I didn't just pray for a wife. I prayed that I would be ready for the relationship when it happened."

While Tim was preparing himself to be the right person for a committed relationship, Joyce was doing the same thing.

"When Tim called me the day after our first date to tell me he didn't want to get too involved, I told him I had something to say," recalls Joyce. "I explained that I had not gone to church looking for a husband. I made sure he understood that I had my own separate relationship with God and my own personal prayer life. I didn't need to ride on his coattails."

"Joyce knew what she wanted," says Tim. "Her self-assuredness became more of an attraction for me than anything else."

After a second phone conversation, Tim and Joyce decided to see each other again, although this time, they met privately.

"We waited two weeks for the talk at church to die down, and then we dated in secrecy," says Tim. "Whenever we were in church together, we pretended we were not in a relationship. We saw each other for an entire year without anyone knowing about it."

When Joyce and Tim finally revealed their clandestine romance, they did so two months before getting married. When they announced their engagement to the entire congregation, they received a standing ovation.

"Everyone in the church embraced us," says Joyce. "We made

sure that we involved the congregation in the planning of the wedding. The women gave me a shower, and the men gave Tim a bachelor party."

Married 17 years, Joyce and Tim agree that the biggest challenge in their relationship has been blending families from previous marriages.

"With the help of premarital counseling and lots of step-parenting books, we worked at showing our children how to stick together as a family," says Joyce. "We cooked together. We ate together. We cleaned together. And, we traveled together."

Although combining two families was a strain on their marriage, the biggest stress on their relationship occurred soon after one of their sons was born. It was at that time in their marriage that Tim received a court letter requesting he take a blood test to confirm that he was the father of a child born to another woman.

One of the reasons the court letter rocked Tim and Joyce's marriage but didn't shatter it was that Tim had been honest with Joyce about the situation before they were married.

"When I proposed to Joyce, I told her up front about another woman I had been in a relationship with after my divorce and who I thought I might have fathered a child with," explains Tim. "I told Joyce that I tried to take responsibility for the child from day one. It wasn't until later in our marriage that I learned I was the father."

"If this had happened and Tim had never told me the truth about the situation, it would have been very tough on our marriage," says Joyce. "Instead, we have accepted the responsibility, and Tim's daughter is an important part of our family."

As parents of five children, Tim and Joyce have learned to balance parenting with their need for time as a couple. They both agree that you must not be so much of a parent that you forget to be a spouse.

Their remedy for tense situations is to get away together.

"I remember when Tim made reservations for us to go away together, but didn't tell me where we were going," says Joyce. "All he said was that I was to go home and quickly pack a bag. I didn't know it, but Tim had reserved us a dinner table and a suite at the Ritz Carlton."

Tim smiles at the memory of their special evening together. What was once this couple's best kept-secret is now common knowledge for all who know them: they are in love.

'Bloom Where You are Planted

SHARON & MIKE HARGROVE

Sitting in Mike and Sharon Hargrove's kitchen makes you feel as warm as a cup of hot cocoa on a blustery winter's day and as comfortable as a pair of favorite bedroom slippers after a 25-mile run. The only thing to rival the welcoming atmosphere of the Hargrove home is the authenticity of its owners.

As the wife of a major league baseball player and former Cleveland Indians manager, Sharon Hargrove has made houses into homes 92 times in 18 different cities and 11 different states. Needless to say, she's good at making herself—and others—feel right at home. The engaging personality reflected in every corner of her family's house in Richfield is also apparent to every person she meets.

"I don't know of anyone who doesn't like Sharon," says Mike. "She is the only person I have ever met who has no agenda at all other than just being who she is."

It was Sharon's "what you see is what you get" personality that drew Mike to her when they met as teenagers at a high school football game in their hometown of Perryton, Texas.

Sharon remembers when someone came up to her at the game to tell her that Mike Hargrove wanted her to sit by him.

"I didn't even know who Mike Hargrove was," says Sharon, "but I agreed to sit next to him because he was cute. We didn't say one word to each other the whole time because Mike was so intent on watching the game. It didn't matter, though. I just cheered with the cheerleaders and laughed at my own jokes."

Mike's memory of their first encounter is slightly different.

"I didn't have to say a whole lot because Sharon was busy talking to everyone around us," recalls Mike. "Sharon has always been outgoing. She can sit and talk to a rock for 15 minutes and get a response out of it. I'm outgoing to a certain extent, but it's harder for me than it is for Sharon to warm up to people."

Although no words were exchanged between Mike and Sharon at the football game, it didn't deter Mike from asking Sharon to go steady before she left the field that day.

This couple continued their romance through high school and afterwards, when they both attended Northwestern Oklahoma State University in Alva, Oklahoma. It was at Northwestern that Mike first played the sport that would change his and Sharon's life forever.

"Even though Mike was courted by Texas A&M to come and play football, Mike chose a smaller school because of the basketball scholarship he was offered," explains Sharon. "At the end of the first basketball season, when the baseball coach asked Mike to come out for the team, Mike told him that he didn't play much baseball. His high school hadn't had a team. After getting encouragement from his dad, Mike joined the baseball team and made All Conference at first base during his first season."

On the heels of Mike's start in baseball came another great beginning—the beginning of Sharon and Mike's lifelong commitment to one another. Mike was 21 and Sharon was 19 when they got married. The summer between Sharon's junior and senior years, they headed to Kansas where Mike played semi-pro ball.

"When we were newlyweds, I watched Mike play baseball from the stands at night and hated it," says Sharon. "I thought the game was so slow and boring. It wasn't until Mike bought me a scorebook and taught me how to keep score that I began to like the game."

The following year, after Mike was drafted by the Texas

Rangers, he and Sharon left for Geneva, New York, where Mike was to play in the New York–Penn minor league. With a $2,000 signing bonus and $100 in cash that Mike's dad had given him, they drove across the country. Their first stop was St. Louis, Missouri.

Having just enough money to buy two barbeque beef sandwiches, a bag of chips, and a Coke to share between them, they walked into Busch Stadium and watched their first major league baseball game.

"I remember looking at Mike during the game," says Sharon. "He was dreamy-eyed. When I asked him what he was thinking, he said, 'I'm thinking that if I have to play 10 years in the minor leagues to play one game on a field like this, it's going to be worth it.'"

After one year in the minor league, a contract that did not include a raise for the next year, and a less than stellar batting average, Mike's optimism took a nosedive. He was ready to hang up his baseball bat and go home.

Sharon remembers that low point for her husband. "Mike looked at me and said, 'I hit .267 in the lowest form of baseball a person can be in professionally. I'm not making any money. We both have college degrees and could get teaching jobs.'

"I told him that he could go ahead and spend the rest of his life wondering if he ever would have made it, but I wasn't going to be married to someone like that."

So with Sharon's faith in him as the fuel to keep him playing, Mike and Sharon headed to Gastonia, North Carolina, where Mike played "A" ball and led the league with a batting average of .351.

After spending time at an instructional camp in Florida, Mike received a letter from the Texas Rangers inviting him to the big league camp for spring training in Pompano, Florida. Following the last exhibition game, Mike approached Billy Martin, the manager of the Texas Rangers, and asked if Martin was planning on sending him to the Double-A or Triple-A league. Billy Martin surprised Mike with the stuff that dreams are made of when he said, "Actually, Mike, I was thinking about sending you to Arlington."

That day happened to be April Fool's Day, so when Mike called Sharon to share the big news, she didn't believe him.

"Because I was a substitute teacher at the time and had already endured endless April Fool's jokes, it took Mike five minutes to convince me he was telling the truth," explains Sharon.

(When I asked Mike's father, Dudley, who happened to be visiting, how he felt when his son told him he had made the big league, he grinned and said, "If I'd had a vest with buttons, I would have popped them.")

Despite the time demands that came with Mike's 31 years of playing baseball or managing teams, this couple has always put their marriage and family first.

Sharon remembers a particular phone call she received from Mike while he was on the road playing with the San Diego Padres and she was a young mother at home with three babies.

"Mike called me from the ballpark in St. Louis and said, 'Sharon, guess what I had for lunch today?' When I heard his voice, I remember thinking, *I didn't have lunch. I'm here by myself with three children. I know no one, and you call me to ask me to guess what you had for lunch today?*

"He proceeded to tell me that he had a barbeque beef sandwich, a bag of chips, and his own Coke from the same place we had shared a Coke seven years before. That phone call was awesome."

Although Mike and Sharon work hard at spending as much time together as possible, this past year has been particularly hard on their relationship. An illness of a family member, as well as a death in the family, caused them to be apart for six weeks, the longest they have ever been separated.

"Because of the distance between us and not being able to spend time together, this year has been the toughest year," says Mike, "but I've never entertained the thought of our marriage not working."

One of the things Sharon has done to ease the pain of her husband's absence, for herself and especially for her children, has been to create a chain of paper links representing the number of days until Mike's return. With each passing day, a link is torn off until there are no more links and Mike is back home.

Although Sharon's original dream was to someday marry and raise a family in her hometown of Perryton, Texas, her mother gave her a piece of advice that has stood her in good stead through her 92 moves.

"My mom always told me to bloom where I was planted or transplanted," says Sharon. "She would say, 'Sharon, God is going to put you where you need to be and it's your job to bloom there.'"

When asked what makes their relationship work so well, Sharon and Mike reflect on their 33 years of marriage and point to a mutual value: family.

"We both come from really good families who loved each other a bunch," says Mike. "When we first got married and began to have children, we made a commitment to each other that our family would always be together, regardless of where my career would take us."

"For as long as I can remember, Mike has felt that baseball has been his livelihood, but not his life," says Sharon. "Baseball has been a way for him to provide for his family first, and a way to enjoy a career second."

As a testament to their strong family values, all five of Sharon and Mike's children live in the Cleveland area.

"Family is all-important," insists Mike. "If you don't have family, then what else is there? Everybody needs a place to go when things aren't working, no matter how old you are. The basis for the strength in our marriage is that our family is a safe haven for everything."

Blending Their Voices for Change

Nina McLellan & Walter Nicholes

When Nina McLellan and Walter Nicholes exchanged wedding vows on June 16, 1990, they did more than publicly declare their love and their devotion to one another. They proclaimed their personal convictions and collective vision for a better world.

In the presence of family and friends, this couple spoke of their commitment to economic and racial justice, their quest for world peace, and their respect for differences between individuals. On their wedding day, Nina and Walter not only embarked on a life journey ripe with hope and possibilities for their relationship, but also began their marriage with a strategic operating plan to make their community a better place.

Nina, with her professional background in human services planning and program development, is an organizer and strategist. Walter is an experienced public relations and advertising professional. Combined, they are a dynamic team working to effect social change while dealing with the issues of war, nuclear weapons, social justice, and human rights.

"When we first met in the early '70s, we were married to other people," says Nina. "We had joined a group called Heights Citizens for Human Rights, a local organization dedicated to racially

169

integrating the Heights area. Walter and I have been social justice activists all our adult lives, so it was likely we would eventually meet each other there."

Years later, when Walter and Nina were divorced from their former spouses, they would see each other at various demonstrations. Finally, at a 1983 fundraising concert for Cleveland Sane Freeze, an anti–nuclear weapons organization, Walter decided to invite Nina on a date.

"It was like being a kid again," says Walter. "I thought I would ask Nina to the movies, but worried about what would happen if she turned me down."

Nina accepted Walter's invitation to the movies and, afterwards, his invitation to go sailing. In turn, she invited Walter to a Sierra Club outing, and for the next few months, they shared biking, hiking, and cross-country skiing while living busy professional lives. Nina worked full time as a senior planning associate at the Federation for Community Planning, and Walter was vice president for corporate communications with a Nestlé food-service subsidiary.

"Dating each other was like being put through an indoctrination course," says Walter. "We had to make sure we liked all of the same outdoor activities."

"Both of us are very physical people," says Nina. "We don't feel good unless we've biked, hiked, walked, skied, or done something physical every day."

Though Walter and Nina share many interests, ice hockey—which Walter played as a boy—is one activity Nina doesn't participate in. During their dating years, though, Nina would listen to Walter talk about his love of the sport.

"He talked and dreamed about his childhood ice hockey experience," explains Nina. "But the only time he ever actually skated was as a young boy playing 'pickup' with other kids on small country ponds during winters in New York State. He never forgot those thrilling days."

Now 79 years old, Walter has participated in a hockey league for 10 years, and he has his wife to thank for it. At Walter's retirement party, Nina gave him a pair of skates, a hockey stick, a puck, and encouragement to live his dream.

"He's a natural," boasts Nina. "In terms of endurance, strength, and energy, Walter is incredible. He has had a life that would have defeated most people. As a young child, he experienced several life-threatening situations and then saw action in World War II. Because of that, he came into adulthood with emotional wounds that, with therapy, took some time to heal. My understanding of this helps when we have our tense times."

Nina is quick to admit that although she may be the calmer of the two, she struggles with the all-important relationship skill of setting boundaries. For her, saying "No" to people in her life is often difficult.

"Walter helped me realize that it's okay to be appropriately angry," says Nina. "He was a major help to my learning when I should set boundaries and say 'No.'"

The balance this couple strikes between emotion and intellect in their relationship is similar to their balanced attitude toward life in general. They are intense when it comes to their work with social justice issues. However, when they are not vigorously working toward peace and justice, they are taking time to enjoy the simple things in life.

"We take life very, very seriously sometimes, and at other times we take the joys and pleasures that life can give us," says Walter.

For this couple, one of those pleasures is opera, light opera in particular. When asked to recall one of their most romantic memories, the aria "My Hero" from *The Chocolate Soldier* by Oscar Straus comes to mind.

"We were at Walter's nephew's farm in the Catskills, standing in a clean, clear, trout-filled mountain stream when Walter said that if I'd sing "My Hero" to him, he'd marry me on the spot. His son, Paul, was with us that day and knew the standard wedding text of the Episcopalian wedding ceremony. He agreed to preside and be our witness."

As if standing in that same stream together, Nina and Walter gaze into each other's eyes and begin to sing, *Come, come, I love you only. You are divine!*

Neither has to struggle to remember the lyrics of the aria, for the memory of their most romantic moment together resurrects the words that were sung and the feelings that were shared on the farm that day.

Whether blending their voices for love, peace, or social justice, this couple realizes their marriage is a partnership, the mission of which is to improve not only the state of their union, but also the state of the world.

"Divorce is Not a Failure"

CINDY & MARK BROWN

When Cindy and Mark Brown found each other, they hadn't been looking. Both married once before for almost the same number of years, they were on separate spiritual paths when they met—paths they later realized were destined to cross.

Mark Brown has a different perspective on divorce than you might expect from a psychologist who's also a marriage and family therapist. When a husband and wife who are struggling in their marriage come to see him, he always goes the conservative route first and does all that he can to help them stay together. If the couple decide they want to get divorced, however, Mark helps them see the hidden gifts that he believes lie within their decision. Through his guidance and the use of a book he has written and published, called *The Hidden Gift in Divorce—How to Find Hope, Healing and Spiritual Growth When Your Marriage Ends*, Mark encourages people to view their divorce as a transition rather than an ending.

"Divorce is not a failure," says Mark. "It's a natural process of change that can allow men and women to go to new levels of growth. Instead of coming out of it as a failure, they can come out of it being more than they've ever been before. If people can view their divorce from this perspective rather than being blinded by fear, anger, or guilt, I think they have a chance to see that what they are going through is happening for a purpose."

This perspective, which Mark insists grows from a spiritual outlook, is not something he learned in his doctorate program at Kent State University or while working in a mental health center in southern Ohio. The way he looks at divorce comes from personal experience.

Married 22 years, Mark separated from his wife in June of 1992 and divorced in 1993. During that time, he embarked on a spiritual journey. While on that journey, he met a man named Buzz Meyers, an astrologer who had a gift for much more than astrology. He was known for helping people develop spiritually.

"I remember Buzz telling me that I would meet a woman after December 26th of the next year," says Mark, "and that she would be a very important person in my life. I listened to him but was skeptical."

In the spring of 1994, Mark met another man, named Greg Kehn, a spiritual medium who told him that not only would he soon meet a woman, but he would also change residences.

That summer, Mark's landlord told him he had to move because the property he was living in was being sold. The next day, Mark decided to knock on the door of a beautiful farmhouse he had admired every day on his way to work. He asked the owner if she ever rented space in the structure and was shocked when she said, "Actually, our tenant of 12 years just told us he is moving."

"I was in that place two weeks later," says Mark. "So I moved from a dark basement apartment that I considered a monk's cell to a place on 110 acres that was as light as could be. Every day I was able to walk in the woods and commune with deer and foxes. It was so cool."

While Mark was spending time alone on a vast amount of land, the woman he was to meet a few months later was going through a spiritual awakening of her own, 5 years after leaving her marriage of 21 years.

"I did not have a clue what I was doing when I left my marriage," says Cindy. "I left my marriage because I was driven to do it. I floated and floundered, but grace carried me through. When I met Mark, everything came together. I remember feeling some shame and discomfort about the divorce, but Mark would tell me I was a hero for following my gut feelings faithfully. Mark's perspective on divorce changed everything for me."

At the time Cindy met Mark, she was working at the county board of mental retardation as a case manager. When a coworker told her about the wonderful man she was dating, Cindy asked if he had a brother. Her friend's eyes lit up as she said, "Yes, he does. His name is Mark, and he's weird like you!"

"My nickname at work was Moonbeam," says Cindy. "People I worked with thought I was 'out there' because I was always chasing after spirituality. I had a lot of sacred practices, ways I would connect with God and nature."

A couple of months later when Mark called Cindy, he thought she was anything but weird. The first time they met, they went for a walk at the farm where Mark lived. What was intended to be a one-hour walk turned into a seven-hour walk that included a trek into Chagrin Falls and a hike to the South Chagrin Reservation, after which they went back to his place on the farm.

"I remember, I was standing in Mark's living room and he gave me a hug," says Cindy. "That was my moment. I felt like I melted right into him."

Mark enjoyed his time with Cindy but was somewhat skeptical about the relationship.

"I wasn't afraid," says Mark. "I felt that I was pretty whole and self-contained, and if someone was going to join me, that person was going to have to be pretty whole and self-contained too. Because I felt sure of myself, I wanted to make sure that the light I saw in Cindy wasn't my light being reflected, but her own light."

Although there was no question that Mark was attracted to Cindy, what kept him in the relationship was the spiritual guidance he had received from Buzz Meyers and Greg Kehn. Much of what they had predicted would happen in Mark's life had come to pass, so Mark was willing to bet on the relationship. Thirty days later, he cashed in on his bet when he and Cindy decided to live together on the farm.

"The following February, we went to Sedona, Arizona, and while we were there, we bought our wedding rings, made by Navajo Indians," recalls Mark.

Still not 100 percent sure about a formal commitment, Mark and Cindy put the wedding rings away when they returned home. Ten months later, they took them out and became engaged.

"When Mark proposed, it was the winter solstice," recalls Cindy. "We were in the middle of a field on the farm at two o'-clock in the morning, along with my dog, Sadie.

"I remember Mark saying, 'In the presence of Mother Earth and Sadie, would you be my wife?' I said, 'Is God here too?' When he said 'Yes,' I said 'Okay, I'll marry you.'"

Cindy and Mark's wedding was as simple and homegrown as the proposal.

"We had written our own ceremony and vows," explains Mark. "We walked out to the daisy-filled meadow surrounded by trees and were married by a minister from a Unity Church in Tallmadge. Our choir was a red-tailed hawk sitting up in the trees screaming. It was so cool."

Their vows to one another were as much a commitment to their spiritual paths as they were a commitment to each other.

Mark's vows to Cindy:

Dearest Cindy,

I have come to this meadow to marry you. I have considered this choice consciously, and I have no hesitation in choosing you to be my wife.

I vow to be as kind and gentle with you as I am able, to be honest with you regarding what I think and feel, and to listen to you with an open mind and an open heart.

My intention toward you is to be your partner for the rest of my life, to remain dedicated to you through all times and circumstances over the years, to nurture you in our old age, and to see you off with the greatest care if that prospect comes to pass.

What I have taught you is a new level of intimacy with Mother Earth. What I have learned from you is to speak to God. These we now share as perhaps the most abiding legacy of our time together so far.

I have the deepest gratitude to God and to Spirit that you have come into my life. I cherish you as a gift of the highest order.

I ask you simply, Cindy, if you will be my wife . . .

Cindy's vows to Mark:

In the presence of our loving God, standing firmly on Mother Earth, and in recognition of Spirit as our true guide, I accept you as my husband and offer myself as your wife.

I promise to love you unconditionally and to nurture you in your chosen path.

I promise to be present in our marriage and to see our marriage in the present.

I promise to see you in the fullness of your spirit and to hear you in your own words.

I promise to be true to myself and to share myself with you in fearless, scrupulous honesty.

I promise to share the tasks of everyday life joyfully and I accept all our children as an integral part of our union.

And if you should ever need to leave, I promise to release you completely with blessings for your continued journey.

I promise you these things in light of the abundance, blessedness, and sanctity of this day.

Married seven years, Mark and Cindy live a simple life. The walls in their home are, for the most part, bare so that their eyes may be drawn to the large picture windows and what lies beyond them.

Cindy enjoys living simply. "I have to have color around me, but other than that, you'll see there is nothing on the walls. If I want to look at something beautiful, I look out the window."

Aside from living a simple life, Mark feels that what makes their marriage work so well is that he and Cindy respect each other's spiritual and professional paths. Mark believes that in the best of marriages, couples must do what he calls "individuate." In his opinion, partners must step back from one another and from their marriage in order to discover who they are as individuals from the inside out. Doing so allows each of them to have something more meaningful. It allows them to have a spiritual path—the true hidden gift.

Politically Connected

JANE CAMPBELL &
HUNTER MORRISON

The year was 1977. The place was a campaign headquarters in the old Woolworth's building on Euclid Avenue, where Jane Campbell and Hunter Morrison worked to get Ed Feighan elected as mayor of Cleveland.

"I remember watching this wildly energetic young lady walk in and begin talking with several Cleveland State University folks," says Hunter.

"During that campaign I was knocking on doors to get the word out, and Hunter was writing speeches," says Jane. "They called him 'Handsome Hunter.' Everybody talked about this walk-away gorgeous guy. All of the women around the campaign were desperately falling in love with him. I had to check this guy out. I have to admit, he was pretty cute."

Although Jane and Hunter grew up fairly close to one another, with Hunter attending University School and Jane attending Shaker Heights High School, their five-year age difference kept their paths from crossing until their education was complete.

"Our first substantive conversation was at the reception for Mayor Kucinich's police chief, who had been imported from San Francisco. Jane and I wound up sitting together on the platform."

Although Hunter and Jane engaged in conversation that day, it wasn't until later, when they began to bump into each other at fundraisers for Tim Hagan, Ed Feighan, and Tim McCormick, that they began to socialize. Somewhere during a six-month period of attending fundraising dinners together, a growing attraction sprouted between them. During that time, it wasn't uncommon for them to attend a fundraising dinner and dine at a pizza parlor afterwards.

Having had enough of post-fundraising pizza, they decided to add a bit of romance to their courtship.

"One of our first memorable dates was when we attended a 1940s revue at the State Theatre called 'Stompin' at the State,' recalls Hunter. "We had a corner table in the lobby of the theater amidst the romantic decay."

"Reviving Playhouse Square seemed like a great idea," says Jane. "We were both really drawn to the idea of restoring the playhouses."

When Jane and Hunter first dated, they spent a lot of time in what they felt was another romantic setting. Jane lived in an apartment above a bar on 128th and Buckeye Road. She and Hunter would spend hours sitting on her patio drinking tea and looking down at the town.

"It could have been a Tennessee Williams set," remembers Hunter. "But for the trolley cars and the seamed nylon stockings, everything else was there."

From 1979 to 1982, Jane traveled around the country working to pass the Equal Rights Amendment, using Washington, D.C., as her base. Meanwhile, Hunter was busy working for the city as a young planning director and earning an executive MBA at Cleveland State University.

Although apart from each other much of the time, they stayed in contact by writing letters. For Jane, deciphering Hunter's handwriting was not always easy.

"Hunter's handwriting is a challenge," admits Jane. "To this day, when he writes a grocery list, I have to pray that I buy something close to what is on the list."

After they had dated for seven years, Hunter picked one of the most romantic places on the planet to propose to Jane: St. Bart's, a French island in the Caribbean. The weather was perfect, the scenery was perfect, but Hunter readily admits that the proposal was less than perfect.

"I had this whole romantic idea," explains Hunter. "I even found a restaurant up on a hill where I was going to propose, and then the night before I was going to ask Jane to marry me, we got into a conversation where I ended up being forward and direct rather than romantic."

Jane chuckles as she thinks back on the proposal. "I remember Hunter saying, 'Okay, what do you think? What are we going to do with this relationship? Do you think we should get married?' and me saying, 'I don't know. What do you think? Should we get married?' and us both finally saying, 'Yeah, I think we should.'"

On December 8, 1984, a month after Jane was elected to the state legislature, she and Hunter were married. Nineteen years later, they reflect back on that time in their lives and wonder what they could have possibly been thinking.

"Only someone who had never before done an election or a wedding would have done what we did," says Jane. "We wanted to set a date for our wedding that was after the November 6 election but would allow us enough time to go away for a honeymoon and be back before Christmas."

After Jane was voted into office, a friend brought to her attention the fact that invitations had not yet been addressed and mailed for a wedding that was to occur in one month.

"The committee to elect Jane Campbell suddenly became the committee to marry Jane Campbell," says Jane.

"Those were the days before computerized mailing lists," says Hunter. "A friend of ours opened up her home so that we could enlist revolving teams of people to help address the invitations."

An assembly line is not usually needed to address wedding invitations, unless, of course, hundreds of guests are on the guest list.

"We invited 400 people," says Jane. "The interesting thing is that 700 people came. We were married at Trinity Cathedral and had an all-church reception there. A dinner party was given for a smaller group of people after the church reception."

Whether in their professional lives as mayor of Cleveland and city planner of Youngstown, or in their personal lives as husband and wife and active parents of two daughters, this Cleveland couple is accustomed to commitment as standard operating procedure.

"My personal role model for commitment and steadfastness is my father, who did not divorce my mother even though she was a raging alcoholic," says Hunter. "After 15 to 20 years of drinking, my mother went into recovery in 1965, when I was 17. Her story is one of hopefulness, and proof that families can repair."

An incredibly engaging and bright woman, Hunter's mother was one of the pioneers in family intervention. She eventually earned a master's degree in social work with a specialization in working with alcoholics.

"My father supported my mother in her recovery and in her getting a graduate degree," says Hunter. "He would go to the Alcoholics Anonymous meetings with her and watch as she'd take in families in different stages of disarray. The key lesson for me occurred years later when I asked my father if he had ever considered getting divorced. He told me that it had never crossed his mind. He said that when he took that vow, he meant what he said."

Hunter and Jane are continually reminded of Hunter's mother's positive influence. While at Playhouse Square a year ago, they were approached by a stranger who told them how Hunter's mother had saved her life and the life of her family.

"That level of commitment is what love is all about," says Hunter.

When thinking about his devotion to Jane, Hunter becomes philosophical.

"There was a time in my relationship with Jane when I imagined myself being 85 years old and wondering if she would be someone I'd want to be with. I realized that like a single malt whiskey, she is an acquired taste."

Jane laughs at the analogy and says, "Actually, I *am* an acquired taste. Not many people could put up with me. I mean, really. Who wants to be my husband?"

As mayor of Cleveland, Jane keeps a grueling schedule. With a police officer posted outside of her home 24 hours a day and a personal driver assigned to transport her to and from meetings, interviews, and a myriad of other commitments, she maintains a hectic and exciting lifestyle.

"When you date and court a political fundraiser and marry someone who is in the business, it's like being in the theater," says Hunter. "You realize going into it that there's a set of demands. That's just part of the gig."

More Than a Matter of Degrees

SYLVIA & AL RIMM

In every healthy marriage, a couple shares the most basic of values. Of the many values a couple may espouse, there is always one that is predominant. For the Rimms, that value is education.

Born of immigrant parents who moved from Riga, Latvia, to Perth Amboy, New Jersey, at the height of the Depression, Sylvia frequently heard her mother and father say, "In America, ve can vork our vay up!"

Because her older sisters hadn't gone to college, Sylvia hadn't expected to either.

"It was my high school guidance counselor, Henrietta Herbert, who said to me, 'Sylvia, you can go to college!'"

After applying for scholarships and receiving more than she could use, Sylvia chose to attend Douglass College, the women's college of Rutgers University in New Jersey. While there, she met her husband, Al.

Al attended Rutgers, three miles across town. One evening in 1954, Al's roommate, Barry, suggested that the two of them go to Douglass College to meet a friend of his girlfriend.

"My friend Carolyn, Barry's girlfriend, had set the meeting up without me knowing about it," remembers Sylvia. "After we met, Al and I talked briefly, but that was it. I didn't think much of it until a few weeks later when I got a call from him at eleven o'clock

at night asking me to go to a Princeton–Rutgers football game
and to dinner."

Carolyn and Barry accompanied Al and Sylvia to the game that
day. From a conversation Sylvia had with Barry, Al learned how
truly important education was to her.

"Barry wanted Carolyn to marry him two years before she
would have graduated from college," explains Sylvia. "I didn't
think that was right. I told him I thought he should let Carolyn
graduate from college before they got married. Although what I
said may have been perceived as a gutsy thing to say, to me, it
seemed logical. There was no way I was going to get married until
after I graduated from college, and there was no way I would have
married someone who didn't want me to complete college."

After the football game, Al and Sylvia went to dinner alone and
later spent hours talking and walking. During their conversations,
it became increasingly clear to Sylvia that Al wanted to be with a
woman who cherished education and planned on using her
schooling to build a career once children were raised.

"At that time, many men would have been threatened by their
wives having a career, but with Al, I never had to worry about
that," says Sylvia.

After a year and a half of dating, Al proposed to Sylvia in a creative and somewhat cryptic way. For Sylvia's birthday during their
first year together, Al gave her a book. For her next birthday, he
gave her a record of Beethoven's Ninth Symphony, along with a
card. In the card he had drawn a picture of a book, a record
album, and an engagement ring. Although the drawings were
primitive, Sylvia got the message. A year and a half later, they were
married.

Once they were wed, Al earned a master's degree prior to
spending a year in the air force, after which he earned a Ph.D.

"I had majored in agriculture as an undergraduate and in 1960
earned a Ph.D. in dairy genetics. Because I couldn't find a job in
that field, I went into medicine as a biostatistician and later became self-trained in epidemiology."

Al's career took Sylvia and their children to 17 different locations until they settled on a farm in the Midwest while Al worked at the Medical College of Wisconsin in Milwaukee for 26 years.

"One of the things we wanted in our life was to live in a geographically beautiful and restful environment. The farm became very important to us for that reason," says Sylvia.

"As a family, we planted 10,000 apple trees on our land," explains Al. "In Madison, there was a farm market around the capital building, and every Saturday we used to go there and sell apples and cider. Sylvia was the best apple seller there ever was."

Although today Sylvia talks about life on a farm as a lifestyle she treasured, she admits that the thought of living on acres of land did not always appeal to her.

"Al told me on our first date that he wanted to live on a farm someday, and it scared me," recalls Sylvia. "I had grown up in a small city in New Jersey in a lower-income neighborhood and was a fearful kid. I remember running up our block being scared to death that strange men were following me. The thought of living on a farm really frightened me."

Al's dream of owning a farm made Sylvia fearful at first, but it didn't take her long to overcome her trepidation.

"I always felt safe with Al and knew he would protect me," says Sylvia. "I not only trusted him completely, I admired him for his breadth of knowledge and for his great sense of humor. I was very serious and needed somebody to laugh with."

"Don't believe a word she's saying," interrupts Al. "You know what attracted her to me? My curly hair."

True, Sylvia has appreciated her husband's hair and sense of humor, but she has valued his infinite support of her career as well. While Al enjoyed a full professorship at the Medical College of Wisconsin, he encouraged Sylvia as she steadily built her own reputation. The director of four clinics with a total staff of 17 people, she became extremely successful and quite well known as an author, a professor, and a parenting expert.

"Sylvia was the best-known woman in Wisconsin," asserts Al. "I'd cash a check anywhere and I'd be asked, 'Who are you?' When I'd say 'Sylvia Rimm's husband,' that was all I'd have to say."

So in 1992, when Al received a letter from a search committee at Case Western Reserve University asking him to interview for chairman of a department at the school, Sylvia wasn't the least bit interested in leaving Wisconsin.

"I remember telling Al that if he wanted to interview for the job he could go ahead and do that, but I didn't want to leave," says Sylvia.

"When I was offered the job at Case, I explained to the dean that my wife had a Ph.D. and was very successful. I told him that I wouldn't come to Cleveland unless they found her a job. When the dean asked me to fax him Sylvia's résumé, I said, 'Well, I could do that, but it's 37 pages long.' Soon after, Sylvia was hired at MetroHealth Medical Center."

Although she had no reputation in the city of Cleveland when she arrived in February of 1993, it didn't take Sylvia long to build one. As a monthly guest on the *Today* show for nine years, the host of a weekly one-hour public radio program broadcast nationally from Cleveland, an author, and a syndicated newspaper columnist, Sylvia quickly became a celebrity.

Clevelanders for 10 years now, Sylvia and Al enjoy their Sheffield Lake home. Admittedly, they have given up the beautiful, restful environment of their Wisconsin farm to settle here. They have replaced it, however, with an environment that is no less peaceful and beautiful. Built within yards of the Lake Erie shore, this couple's home provides tranquility as well as drama. With windows that span the width of their house, they relish a spectacular view during every season of the year.

After 46 years of marriage and several postgraduate degrees between them, education has not only been a priority for Sylvia and Al as individuals, it has been fundamentally important to their children as well.

"We have four children who have six doctorate degrees," says Al.

"Two of our children have M.D.s and Ph.D.s, and the other two have Ph.Ds.," explains Sylvia.

Although they are clearly committed to higher learning, Al and Sylvia credit their long marriage to more than a passion for education.

"Having the same core values is most important," says Sylvia. "A good marriage always develops new interests, but if you have the same core values, then you'll be able to support each other through life. In our family, core values included a strong work ethic and education, balanced by plenty of family togetherness and laughter."

As Al reflects back on their life together, he smiles. "Sylvia was raising four kids, going to graduate school getting a Ph.D., and was married to a crazy husband. And she got through it. That pretty much wraps up our life together."

Sylvia chuckles and admits, "It's never been boring."

Hope Is a Decision

MARYANN & DICK MCKENNA

When asked why he works his muscles every day, Christopher Reeve has been quoted as saying "because I want my body to be able to accept the cure when it comes."

Dick McKenna derives hope and inspiration from Reeve's attitude. After 29 years of marriage and 52 years of life, Dick was diagnosed with multiple sclerosis.

"Dick's disease is progressive," says Maryann, "but the symptoms were dormant for many years."

As a young man, Dick was in a car accident and was thrown from the automobile. Afterwards, while training to become a commercial pilot, he lost some of his eyesight in one eye and was unable to continue to pursue his dream of flying. Dick assumed his loss of sight had been caused by the car accident and was surprised when the doctors told him 30 years later that the loss of vision was a symptom of multiple sclerosis.

"In my late forties, I began to have a lot of pain in my back and had trouble walking," explains Dick. "For many years before that, I had been off balance and kind of klutzy. I thought it had to do with my not seeing well out of one eye."

For Dick's particular type of progressive MS, there are no medications. Even if there were, he is not sure he would take them.

"Even if there was a medication that would slow down my progression, there are too many side effects involved," says Dick. "I've tried to take a different path to healing. I've been studying since 1997 about the nervous system and how the mind and emotions can affect the body. What I have found is that emotions are physical. Anytime we have an emotion, there is biochemistry which, when released in the brain, goes to targeted cells. Therefore, our emotions can improve or diminish our health."

From Maryann's perspective, how she thinks about her husband's disease is everything. With three boys to raise, a home to maintain, and a job to get to, life must go on. Looking back on her life with Dick, Maryann feels that her marriage has not been any the worse for wear.

"Dick's disease has limited some of the things that we do, such as going to restaurants we used to go to, but we have found other restaurants and do other things. Malls are a great place to go because they are so handicapped accessible," says Maryann. "I believe that if you let the disease take over your life, it's because you've decided to allow it to take over."

Dick is grateful for Maryann's resolute nature.

"When I first started to have a problem, we experienced a role reversal," says Dick. "Maryann became the major breadwinner and finally the only breadwinner. I really admire her for the way she just picked up where I left off and did what she had to do."

"I have to admit, I am a natural caretaker," says Maryann. "But when I want to go out with my girlfriends, I go. Dick has always been great about me doing what I need to do for me. He would never tell me I couldn't do anything or go anywhere."

Between the years of 1995 and 1999, Dick went from using a cane to using a walker, and finally a wheelchair. His growing dependence upon aids to keep him mobile did not prevent this North Olmsted couple from traveling, however. Over the years, they have spent time in the Caribbean, most recently in St. Croix.

"One of my most romantic memories was our first trip to St. Thomas," remembers Maryann. "Dick and a friend of ours planned the trip to celebrate our anniversaries. It was a complete surprise."

Dick recalls a romantic moment that, to this day, makes his heart skip a beat whenever he thinks about it.

"I had gone to Phoenix to take some classes for two weeks, and Maryann came out to meet me halfway through the stay," recalls Dick. "I was using a cane at that time and went into the airport to find her. When I saw her standing in the baggage claim area, it was a great moment. I can still remember what she was wearing."

Experiences that have helped this couple sustain their strong marriage include participating in a Marriage Encounter weekend and teaching Pre-Cana classes (church-sponsored sessions in which married volunteers share their insights on marriage with engaged couples). The Marriage Encounter weekend, in particular, helped them get through one of the toughest periods in their relationship.

"Throughout most of our marriage, Dick has had problems with starting businesses," says Maryann. "With business loans and the uncertainty of a salary based on commission, we had a lot of financial stress."

One of the things that helped Maryann and Dick discuss their money issues was the idea that feelings are not right or wrong. They just are.

"One of the best things we did during those times," says Dick, "was to talk about talking. Maryann has always been able to talk about her feelings and has taught me how to do the same thing."

Humor is a linchpin in this couple's marriage. With the day-to-day struggle to stay positive, fend off boredom, and remain as mobile as possible, it could be easy for Maryann and Dick to lose their ability to see the funny side of life.

"We laugh at the most ridiculous things," says Maryann. "I remember the morning Dick came out of the bathroom after taking a shower. He was wearing only his underwear and sitting in the wheelchair. I noticed his feet were swollen, so I grabbed one foot and then the other to prop them up on the bed. I looked the other way, and all of a sudden I heard Dick saying, 'Hon, oh, Hon.' I turn around and there he is in the wheelchair flat on his back with his feet up in the air."

Married 37 years, Dick and Maryann believe in spreading words of hope. As avid supporters of the MS Society, Dick has given talks at area schools to promote the MS Readathon, and Maryann has participated in the MS Walk for several years.

Whether one of the partners in a marriage is disabled or both are the picture of health, the McKennas' advice to every couple is the same.

"You can't change your partner," says Maryann. "You can only change yourself."

Dick agrees. "The only thing you can change is yourself, and sometimes that changes everything."

Banding Together

TAMAR & LENNY GRAY

When a man and woman meet each other and share a common gift, a talent they know they are destined to use for the rest of their lives, a deep bond can form. That's exactly what happened to Lenny and Tamar Gray.

Both musically gifted, they were mentored and encouraged to pursue their dreams at a very young age. Lenny's fourth-grade teacher recognized his talent for playing the drums, and Tamar's family, all musically gifted themselves, encouraged her to explore a future in music.

"I remember being in a talent show when I was in eighth grade and winning first place," says Tamar. "After that, I was hooked and decided I wanted to attend a high school for performing arts."

"I played my first professional gig at age 14 and made $25," remembers Lenny. "When I started high school, a friend of mine asked me to help him start a soul band. I played drums for a while, then gradually switched to bass."

After receiving her bachelor's degree in music education at the University of Evansville in Indiana, Tamar moved to Columbus, Indiana, in 1985 to begin her teaching career.

"My first husband brought me to Cleveland," explains Tamar. "But looking back on it, we say my first husband brought me to Cleveland to meet my second husband."

Lenny and Tamar met for the first time when Lenny was asked to join a band with Tamar as one of the lead singers. As soon as she stepped onstage, he was taken with her.

"At the time we met, I was single and looking," says Lenny, "but when I heard she was married, I knew she was off limits."

Although Tamar was married at the time, the marriage was beginning to disintegrate.

"I remember the day Lenny and I were sitting in the car together waiting for band practice to start," says Tamar. "I was in the process of a divorce, and Lenny turned to me and said, 'You know, I really like you a lot.' I remember saying, 'Well, that's nice.' And he said, 'No, I mean I really like you.' I told him that at the time I wasn't available to be in a relationship, but he was the most persistent man I had ever met."

Lenny respected the awkward position Tamar was in, but was determined to remain a close friend. During those first few months, they shared their passion for music and their career dreams. It was then they both realized they were more than just friends. They were kindred spirits.

"Over the course of a year, as my marriage was ending, my friendship with Lenny became more and more valuable," says Tamar. "It was very refreshing to know that he was for me all the way, encouraging me and understanding what I do, just as I understood what he does."

Once Tamar was single again, she and Lenny slipped into a relationship that felt only natural. With a relationship based on friendship, a shared musical passion, and love, the foundation had been laid for a permanent future together. One year later, Lenny placed the first brick on that foundation and shocked Tamar with a knock-your-socks-off proposal.

Tamar had just received her master's degree in educational administration from John Carroll University and decided to celebrate by having a huge party with 100 guests. Lenny capitalized on that celebration and used it as a way to propose.

"I was sweating bullets," recalls Lenny. "I decided to give a toast to Tamar and combine it with a marriage proposal. I remember saying, 'Congratulations Tamar for getting your master's. I hope you have a long and successful life.' After everyone clinked glasses, I got down on one knee and said, 'And . . . would you do me the honor of being my wife?'"

The shock hit Tamar full force. For longer than most would have expected, she stood facing Lenny, speechless. Once she finally said yes, all of the women descended upon her.

Tamar admits her slow response to the proposal was not only because of shock, but because of a smidgen of uncertainty as well.

"After you've been in a marriage that has gone bad, you're not always sure about getting married again," explains Tamar. "Before and after Lenny proposed, I told him that he didn't have to marry me. Although I am a firm believer in marriage, I did not want to go through what I had gone through the first time."

A few months later, during their engagement, Tamar's uncertainty evaporated.

"I had been so sick," remembers Tamar. "Lenny came over to my apartment that morning and cooked me breakfast, did my laundry, and made sure I was eating. I realized then what a very special man he was and that I really did want to marry him."

The following summer, on the day of their wedding, Tamar once again got the chance to see why Lenny was a very special man. As guests were arriving, Tamar and Lenny learned that the minister, a friend of theirs, was going to be over an hour late for the wedding because his son was in the hospital having tests. Although there were two other ministers available to conduct the ceremony, Lenny remained calm and secure in his faith that his friend would arrive in due time and would perform the ceremony.

"I remember waiting and crying in the basement of Lenny's mother's house," says Tamar. "I sent a message upstairs to Lenny to grab one of the other ministers to marry us, but he was so calm and self-assured. He had faith and he was right. It all worked out."

Lenny and Tamar consider their faith to be a vital part of their marital success.

"Our religious beliefs are something we both value as individuals and as a couple," says Lenny.

"Putting God into our marriage is very important to us," says Tamar. "As the Bible says, we have to love our neighbor as ourselves. Your spouse is the closest neighbor you're going to have."

Lenny and Tamar feel united in their spirituality but, surprisingly, attend different churches. They have come to realize that going their separate ways on Sunday morning, although perhaps not ideal, is what they each need to do to feed their own souls.

"Lenny is the instrumentalist at Union Congregational Church, and I'm the music director at Edgehill Community Church," explains Tamar. "We've attended each other's services and often enjoy it, but we respect the fact that we get things from our own church that we don't always get from each other's church."

Recently, Lenny and Tamar attended an annual couples retreat at his church where they learned about the concept of submission in a marriage.

"I hate the word 'submission,'" says Tamar. "But at the workshop, they shed a new light on the topic. All I could see when they talked about submission was a man lording it over his wife, and I didn't like it. Now I understand submission to be submitting or surrendering to God, and by doing so naturally submitting to each other. What that means for me is that I don't have to be in control anymore and insist it has to be my way. I've learned to do it Lenny's way sometimes because Lenny does it my way a lot."

This couple knows that when it comes to their relationship, continuing education is paramount. As a couple, they read books on relationships, participate in marriage workshops through their church, and have a minister they feel comfortable turning to for help if they need counseling.

"We enjoy participating in anything that will enhance who we are as individuals," says Tamar, "but enhancing who we are as a couple is even better."

Married five years, Lenny and Tamar agree that music, which brought them together in the first place, has enhanced who they are as a couple. Now performing together in a band they call "Etiquette," they know that their passion for music has a permanent place in their life. Needless to say, it plays backup to their passion for each other.

Don't Let the World Get in the Way

PAT & VIC VOINOVICH

As a senior at Shaw High School during the 1960s, Vic Voinovich spent more time studying a cute girl in his economics class than he did studying economics. That cute girl—Pat—is now his wife.

"Pat was involved in a lot of activities in high school, including secretary on student council," remembers Vic. "I used to watch her get pulled out of class a lot for council activities. I was very impressed that she could just stand up and walk out of the room so often. I fell for her right then and there."

What kept Vic interested enough in Pat to stay in love with her was how he felt about himself when he was with her.

"When I was with Pat, I felt like a million bucks," says Vic. "I went from being a C student to being an A student within a semester. When you become a better person as a result of being with someone else, you know that's real."

"I felt the same way," recalls Pat. "Vic made me love myself more, which is hard to do when you're a teenager with fragile self-esteem. I could see myself through his eyes."

You wouldn't think a marriage based on so much mutual admiration would get a rocky start, but it did. Now married 35 years, Pat and Vic admit that what started as a marriage spawned in high school, full of optimism and fairy-tale dreams, took a nosedive within the first five years of matrimony. Between Vic working and going to school full time and Pat student teaching, they barely saw each other. Throw a newborn into the mix, and marital bliss became a distant dream.

It didn't take Vic and Pat long to realize that they had not had the least bit of training for marriage. The only guides they had on how to be married were the marriages around them, which were not always the best. The fact that they struggled with communication didn't help.

"When Pat talked to me, I would try to talk her out of her feelings," recalls Vic. "She'd tell me that she didn't feel close to me, and I'd say, 'What do you mean, I come home every night, don't I?'"

"I finally stopped talking to him because Vic would intellectualize everything I'd say. After a while, I didn't even bother," says Pat.

Then a miracle happened. That miracle came in the form of a Marriage Encounter weekend held in Erie, Pennsylvania. With encouragement from a couple who had gone through this experience themselves, Vic and Pat took a step into a new arena—a step Vic was determined to prove to Pat they didn't need to take.

"I thought we didn't need help. I thought we had the best marriage there ever was," says Vic.

"*You* thought we had the best marriage there ever was," counters Pat. "I didn't. I saw in our friends something we had lost. A closeness. Our friends sat next to each other and held hands. We weren't doing that anymore. I thought, *I want that.*"

Pat's wish for closeness came true, and she says it's all because of the one thing they learned at their first Marriage Encounter weekend and have practiced ever since. That one thing is called dialoguing, a technique where partners choose a question to answer in the form of a letter. Writing, reading, and discussing each of their letters has been a half-hour daily discipline that Vic and Pat have incorporated into their lives since 1971.

Vic and Pat boast about their exemplary dialoguing record

until they remind themselves of the horrendous five days in their marriage when Pat couldn't dialogue because she was too busy struggling to stay alive.

On January 20, 2001, Pat and Vic were attending President George W. Bush's inaugural ball for the state of Ohio in Washington, D.C., when suddenly she felt faint and passed out. Her fainting spell turned out to be cardiac arrest.

"I remember being inside the convention hall in gridlock traffic surrounded by people watching paramedics slicing my wife's gown off," says Vic. "All I could think was that she was dead and we hadn't said good-bye."

Four days later, Pat Voinovich left the hospital with a pacemaker in her chest and a grateful husband on her arm.

"Every day since that day we left the hospital I feel like I've won the lottery," says Vic. "Through it all, I believed God would find a way when there was no way. My experience has always been that God will make the impossible possible."

Pat and Vic have had more than one opportunity for God to perform miracles in their lives. When their 17-year-old daughter, Christy, was in a head-on car collision and had to have brain surgery, they were told she wasn't expected to live through the night. Vic's response to the prognosis was to ask the doctor to bring her team together so that he could pray over the doctors' hands. In a room alone with them, he prayed that the team of doctors would be guided to use their intellects and medical talents to bring about a healthy outcome for his daughter. The Voinoviches expected a miracle. They got what they expected. Ten days later, Pat and Vic's daughter went home from the hospital. She left with memory and speech problems, but she was alive. Two months later, she started college. Today she has six children.

Whatever trauma occurs in their lives, Pat and Vic say it is their commitment to prayer, daily dialogue, and their Marriage Encounter circle of friends that has made their marriage survive and thrive. To this couple, marriage is a discipline.

"We're like long-distance runners," says Vic. "We have to work out every day. I'd write a dialogue letter before I'd brush my teeth."

One of Pat and Vic's goals has been to pass down to their four children and nine grandchildren their legacy of a happy marriage. Recently, when they heard that one of their grandchildren wanted to know why Grandma and Grandpa were always holding hands, they knew they had done their job.

Love, Vegetarian Style

ANN & CALDWELL ESSELSTYN

No sooner had I driven onto the property of Caldwell and Ann Esselstyn than they stepped outside to greet me. This couple's warm welcome was indicative of their passionate and proactive style. Whether they are spending time with one of their grandchildren or traveling through India giving talks on nutrition, conviction is what drives this husband and wife.

Having both been raised in families where the medical profession was a tradition, they each inherited an adventuresome spirit bound and determined to make the world a better place. Having had a grandfather (Dr. George Crile, Sr.) who founded the Cleveland Clinic, and a father (Dr. George [Barney] Crile, Jr.) who picked up where her grandfather left off, Ann was no stranger to groundbreaking achievement and innovation. So when Es (as she affectionately calls her husband) showed up on her radar screen, she was naturally drawn to him.

Cut from the same dynamic cloth as Ann's father and grandfather, Es was already busy making his own mark, in medicine and even in other areas. While attending Yale University, Es spent three years on the rowing team, which represented the United States in the 1956 Olympic Games. When he entered Western Reserve University School of Medicine, he brought a gold medal with him. Little did he know, however, that while in Cleveland he would claim a much more valuable prize—his wife, Ann.

"As a medical student at Yale, my father had known Ann's father as an undergraduate, so when I arrived in Cleveland her dad invited me for dinner to meet his daughter," remembers Es.

"I was teaching in Cambridge, Massachusetts, at the time," recalls Ann. "But I came home for summers. Essy lived in an apartment where the Cleveland Children's Museum is now located, and I remember finding every excuse to drive by that apartment to try to catch sight of him."

After four years of dating Ann, Es asked her to marry him. When Ann accepted his proposal, she knew she was signing on for a lifetime with someone who was passionate not only about her, but also about his work.

"For good or for bad, Essy has blinders on for whatever his passion is at the moment," says Ann.

As a general surgeon at the Cleveland Clinic, Es was the chairman of the breast cancer task force. Having watched Ann's mother and sister suffer from breast cancer and his father have a heart attack at age 43, he decided to study ways to prevent cancer and heart disease. In his research, he found a direct correlation between the two diseases and a person's diet.

"In the late 1970s and early 1980s, I became so disillusioned with the approach to breast cancer. Throughout the world, there were many places where the incidence of breast cancer was 20 times less frequent than in the United States. In the 1950s the disease was virtually unheard of in rural Japan, but after the Japanese had migrated to the United States, the second generation had the same rate of breast cancer as the people in our country."

It was this compelling evidence that convinced him to make a radical change in his own diet, which subsequently became the foundation for his research. He admits to a time when he ate 12 eggs at once, and sandwiches slathered in peanut butter and mayonnaise.

"I was a major cholesterolholic," confesses Es. "I finally made the switch to a plant-based diet in April of 1984, but I couldn't have done it without Ann's willingness and support."

The dietary changeover was one of the biggest challenges they faced together, but Ann supported her husband in making this major lifestyle change.

"Switching to a plant-based diet was difficult," explains Es. "It doesn't sound like much, but it's huge. It absolutely changed our social relationships. We didn't lose friends, but we took a bit of a beating for it."

What made it easy for Ann to change her eating habits was an unforgettable birthday lunch for an aunt at which deviled eggs, oily salad dressing, and Hough Bakery birthday cake were served.

"I remember getting a phone call from my sister during the lunch telling me she had just been diagnosed with breast cancer. That pushed me over the edge. I ate nothing at that lunch. From that moment on, I changed my eating," says Ann.

What has turned out to be a lifelong crusade for this couple has ended up being, in their opinion, one of the biggest gifts they have given to their children.

"All four of our children have changed their eating to include a mostly plant-based diet," says Ann.

Es grins with pride and says, "Our granddaughter walked by the meat section in the grocery store the other day and announced, 'We don't eat meat!'"

The Esselstyns left not only a dietary legacy to their children, but also a model for commitment between a husband and wife, regardless of life's circumstances.

One of the most difficult times in this couple's marriage was during Es's military service in Vietnam.

"I was pregnant with our last child when Essy went to Vietnam in 1967. It was awful. Unbelievably sad. I remember I kept a blue work shirt of his hanging on the back of the bathroom door. It was always there and it smelled just like him. Then one day, I became so upset because a babysitter washed the shirt by mistake," says Ann.

During their 42 years of marriage, time away from one another has left each of them yearning for the other's return. Ann recalls a trip she took to visit one of her children in California. She remembers finding a poem Es had written to her while she was gone.

"Essy wrote me a special poem," says Ann.

(She jumps up from the couch to find it so she can recite it to me.)

Gone

The flowers in the bathroom are missing.
As you nurture the youngest of your genome,
at night my left hand reaches only white noise.
Your absent warmth a vacuum of reality.
Your daily voice reassures me.
Tonight I rejoice with you again.

They Met in the Personals
. . . and It Worked

NATE & SANDRA BENDER

She is the executive director of the Marriage Coalition, a non-profit organization in Cleveland with a mission to enhance family life by promoting and strengthening marriage, but Sandra Bender says that anyone wondering how to get married shouldn't look to her and her husband Nate for an example.

"How we got married was not the way to have done it," says Sandra. "Our kids were not prepared for it."

Although this couple's one-month engagement period might be considered rather short, it was the 48 hours between the time they set the date and had the actual ceremony that sent them reeling. The idea of getting married quickly was prompted by Nate's brother and sister-in-law who were visiting from Australia.

"I remember sitting with my brother and his wife in Arabica Coffee House when they said, 'While we're here, why don't you get married?'" remembers Nate. "And we said 'Okay.'"

"It was December 31 and I only worked half a day," recalls Sandra "The second half of the day we spent buying me a dress for the wedding, getting the rings, the marriage licenses, and verifying divorces. The following day, January 1, 1987, we got married."

This couple's whirlwind wedding did not reflect the pace of their slow-moving, somewhat tentative courtship, which started when Nate answered Sandra's personal ad in *Cleveland* magazine.

"I figured that I didn't have anything to lose," says Sandra. "I had heard other professional women were meeting men through the personals and marrying them, so with help from a friend, I wrote an ad that read, 'Woman with Ph.D., single parent, Christian, tall, likes outdoor activities,' all the things that generally turn men off."

Nate responded to Sandra's ad by sending a letter to her post office box, with a phone number for her to call if she was interested.

"I remember when I called Nate, I was a little taken aback when he said, 'Which one are you?' but instead of being put off by the fact that he didn't seem impressed with my ad, I communicated very clearly exactly who I was based on the ad I had written."

What Sandra had interpreted as disinterest on Nate's part was not indifference at all, but caution. Having been married to—and divorced from—the same woman twice, Nate was careful about getting involved again.

Their first date, lunch at Earth by April in Cleveland Heights, left them both with distinct impressions of one another. "Ms. Sobriety" is how Nate describes his impression of Sandra at that first encounter.

"She was very somber looking and acting," says Nate. "But she was very easy to talk to."

"He was the biggest guy I had seen in a long time," recalls Sandra. "We talked up a storm."

After their lunch, Sandra handed Nate a flyer promoting a support group for divorced people that she had started at Fairmount Presbyterian Church, and suggested he attend. He followed her advice and became a regular participant, giving them the chance to see each other on a regular basis.

"When the group would go dancing, Nate and I would pair up frequently," remembers Sandra.

"I'd be dancing with another woman and Sandra would cut in. I'll always remember that," says Nate.

Dancing with a group led them to take private dancing lessons that summer. Although their relationship was far from becoming serious at that point, the following October, Sandra brought up the topic of marriage.

"I remember asking Nate if he was interested in marriage and he said 'No,'" says Sandra. "He told me he was interested in a buddy, not marriage. Actually, it was hard to know if we were even a couple for the longest time."

Sandra wanted to talk about having a serious relationship, but Nate wasn't ready to commit until a year later, after they had both participated in a self-help group called the Landmark Forum.

"Up to that point, I felt like I had lived my life waiting for a man to prove to me that I was loveable. What I got from the Forum was that no man could do that for me. I had to do that for myself. So when I no longer looked to Nate to show me I was worthy of love, I think that freed him in the relationship."

"When she declared herself loveable, a wife showed up," explains Nate.

Married 17 years, they say the biggest challenge in their relationship has been blending their two families, which include a daughter and two sons.

"It was having different parenting styles that we found to be most challenging," says Sandra, "and at that time, there were no courses for step-parenting or couples education. We relied on our best friends, who were psychologists and 12 years older than we were. They were a mentor couple for us and saw us through some tough times."

Realizing there was a need for such education, and both being psychologists, Sandra and Nate decided to develop and teach a couples' course called "Recreating Marriage," which led to a book by the same name that Sandra and Nate worked on together.

"Part of the book dealt with the importance of affirmations in marriage, and it occurred to me how important it would be for me to affirm Nate for his parenting," explains Sandra. "Once I did that, he stopped arguing with me and we began working as a team while raising our kids."

Sandra and Nate have a system for resolving conflict in other areas of their life.

"We argue until we give up arguing," admits Sandra.

"We argue like everybody else argues, but we don't sling mud," says Nate. "We realize at some point that arguing is no solution. Then we do what we both do real well. We listen to each other. Listening diffuses the energy of the argument and gives us the ability to understand and appreciate both sides."

As family and marriage therapists, the Benders teach other couples the skill of listening. Discouraged with marital therapy that deals with problems only after they surface, Sandra decided to form an organization that would educate couples, as well as clergy and mental health professionals, on how to prevent divorce not only after problems surface, but before they became problems at all. In January of 1999, the Marriage Coalition was founded.

"That summer I went to the second Smart Marriages conference and brought back some of the programs to Cleveland," says Sandra. "One of those programs was the *prepare/enrich* Marital Inventory and Skills Program, which we use to train clergy and mental health professionals so that they can educate couples."

At the 2002 Smart Marriages conference, an annual meeting of the Coalition for Marriage, Family, and Couples Education, Sandra met with government officials who suggested she apply for a grant to help the Marriage Coalition in Cleveland develop a new program that would educate lower-income, unmarried couples with children on how to have a healthy, intact family. In December of 2002, Sandra received the good news from the Department of Health and Human Services in Washington, D.C., that the Marriage Coalition would be receiving close to $200,000 for their pilot program.

There is no doubt about the Benders' strong commitment to marriage, on both a global and personal level. For them personally, commitment means not only being dedicated to the longevity of their relationship, but supporting each other so they become the best individuals they can be.

"What I love most about Nate is his support and understanding," says Sandra. "He is the ground I walk on. He's the runway that my plane takes off from."

"I'm committed to Sandra being all that she can be," says Nate. "I support her in expressing the fullness of her humanity, and I feel the exact same thing from her."

"We Were Just Buddies"

MELINDA & JIM MANTEL

Melinda Mantel's mother was so sure her daughter would marry a friend from high school that she wrote down her prediction and tucked it away in a dresser drawer. In 1981, her forecast came true.

"We were just buddies as teenagers," remembers Melinda. "We liked each other, but never dated. In fact, for my senior prom, I talked Jim into taking my best friend and doubling with me and my date."

Today Jim and Melinda admit that the reason they had never thought about being more than friends was that they were so different.

"I was a rock-and-roll, long-haired rebel," says Jim. "I didn't like school and broke the rules a lot."

Melinda rolls her eyes. "I was such a goody-two-shoes who never got into trouble. I dressed like a yuppie, and Jim wore nothing but jeans."

As would be expected from two people who were diametrically opposed, Jim and Melinda went separate ways after high school. Although Melinda went to Akron University and Jim stayed home and worked in a heating and air-conditioning business, they remained friends through the two years Melinda was at school. When she returned home to help take care of her father, who had become ill, Jim spent a lot of time visiting her. He can't say exactly when liking Melinda turned into loving her, but Jim distinctly remembers the day he turned to her and said, "I think I want to spend the rest of my life with you."

Around the same time Jim realized he wanted Melinda as his wife, he realized he wanted radio as his career.

"I remember when I discovered I wanted to be in radio," recalls Jim. "Every day, no matter what heating or air-conditioning job I was on, I always listened to the radio while working. I'd hear the voices of on-air personalities and think, 'I can do that!'"

Melinda pushed Jim to follow his dream as he worked during the day and went to broadcasting school at night. After Jim graduated, he and Melinda moved to Midland, Texas, so that Jim could start his career in radio. The dream that Melinda had pushed Jim to achieve unfortunately pushed the two of them into the most difficult period in their marriage.

"We always say that we've been married 22 years, but only the last 10 count," says Melinda.

As a young woman in a strange town with a new baby and a husband who worked 12 to 13 hours a day, Melinda wanted out.

"I remember calling my mother and telling her that I wanted to come home," says Melinda. "She wouldn't let me! She told me that I was married and had to stay with my husband. To this day, I credit her with getting us through the hardest time in our marriage."

With her mother's encouragement, Melinda dug her heels into the Texas soil and faced the problems in their relationship. Jim and Melinda's resolve to work on their marriage began to reverse what felt like a downward spiral, but it was marriage counseling and a Marriage Encounter weekend that really turned the tide for this couple.

"I remember the counselor telling us to sit in a room every day for 20 minutes, look at each other, and talk," recalls Jim. "I swear, to this day, that's the reason why we like spending so much time alone together."

The time this couple does spend together, however, is not the traditional time most couples spend together. As the morning drive-time host for WGAR, Jim leaves for work at 3:00 in the morning to work an on-air shift from 5:00 to 9:00. He gets home at 1:30 in the afternoon, and by 9:30 at night he is in bed.

"One thing I always make sure I do," says Melinda, "is go to sleep with Jim every night, even if it is at 9:30. If I didn't do that, I'd never be with him. In the 22 years we've been married, we haven't missed a night of going to bed together."

When asked how they are most alike, this couple laughs and simultaneously says, "We're not!"

In some ways, this Akron couple is as different as they were in high school. Jim loves to ski. Melinda hates cold weather. Jim doesn't like to get dressed up for dinner. Melinda loves formal dining, especially on cruise ships. Melinda saves everything. Jim doesn't. When it comes to decorating, Melinda likes the extras that make a house a home. Jim is bare-bones functional.

"People sometimes say to me, 'The two of you are so different. We can't believe you're still together,'" says Melinda.

But Jim and Melinda know exactly why they are still together. They genuinely like each other.

"The key to our liking each other is that we were friends first and knew each other's faults before we ever started dating," explains Melinda. "Whereas in some marriages, the passion decreases over the years, ours has increased because passion wasn't the only thing that brought us together in the first place. It was our friendship."

With more than 22 years of friendship under their belt, this couple decided it was time to bridge the gap between their likes and dislikes and find something they could enjoy doing together. Sailing has become that bridge.

Putting a boat on the water and making it sail in an agreed-upon direction is no easy task. Tempers can flair. Frustrations can mount. The end result can be a stormy voyage even on the calmest of waters.

"We get along so well when sailing, it's kind of scary," says Melinda.

After sailing lessons in Annapolis and a few trips to the British Virgin Islands with friends and family, Jim and Melinda now make the trip alone together.

With their two daughters almost up and gone, the traditional image of an empty-nest couple sailing off into the sunset seems to apply to Melinda and Jim Mantel.

Happy Being Different

BEN & JUDY SHEERER

As a teenager, Judy spent a lot of time at Ben's house—much of it with curlers in her hair. She and Ben's sister Robin were best friends in high school. Judy and Robin would sit around and talk about a topic commonly discussed by young women in the late 1950s—the topic of marriage.

"In my era, girls started talking about getting married at the age of 17," explains Judy. "If you weren't married by age 19 or 20, people thought you would most likely be an old maid."

When people asked Judy what man she had her sights set on marrying, she would tell them she was interested in either of two men. One of those men was Ben Sheerer.

"I wanted a man who was kind, decent, and thoughtful toward women," explains Judy. "As I learned more about Ben, I realized that not only did he seem like he fit the profile of the man I wanted to marry, he in fact was the man I wanted to marry."

Currently a lawyer in a small Cleveland law firm with which he has been associated for most of his career, Ben has always had a quiet demeanor. Shy as he may appear, his sense of humor makes itself evident through an unmistakable twinkle in his eye.

"Ben was very quiet, but I always enjoyed his sense of humor and liked the air he had about him," says Judy.

It was while waiting at a train station for Ben's sister, Robin, to

arrive home from college that Judy and Ben spent time talking
and realized they quite possibly could have a future together.
They discussed many things that afternoon, including Judy's cur-
rent job and her involvement in community theater.

When Ben asked her, "What would you do if you were interested in a man who didn't like the fact you were in theater?" Judy
didn't have to think twice about her answer. "I'd drop him," she
responded. That was all Ben had to hear to know he would support Judy in her theatrical interests, date her, and eventually
marry her, which he did in 1962.

After performing in a few plays as a young woman, Judy didn't
pursue a theatrical career. Instead she transferred her stage presence and flair for the dramatic to another kind of theater—the
political theater.

"Nothing made me feel more alive than politics," says Judy.

So 10 years after she and Ben were married, when the McGovern campaign office in Cleveland needed a statewide staffer, Judy
zealously stepped forward. She remembers that experience as
being one of the best times of her life.

"I used to wake up in the morning and bound out of bed to be
down at campaign headquarters at seven-thirty in the morning,"
says Judy. "Ben couldn't have been more supportive of me being
involved. He never uttered a single complaint about when and
where I'd be all day and evening."

"Judy has a lot of talent," says Ben. "She is highly organized. I
was happy to stay home and take care of our daughter, Morgan,
who was eight years old at the time. While Judy was at headquarters, Morgan spent time making campaign posters. One of our fa-
vorites, and one that ended up being displayed in the office, read,
"Crackers On Nixon. McGovern's The One."

When the campaign was over and Nixon took office, Judy
spent the next two to three years finishing college and in 1975
graduated with a degree in economics from Cleveland State University. Although she began graduate school immediately, the
more time she spent in the field of economics, the more her enthusiasm for it waned.

"In 1976, a friend came to me and suggested I think about running for office by challenging a sitting state senator, Tony Calabrese. I did that and almost beat him, but he won by two percentage points. Although I lost the election, I knew that I wanted to stay in politics."

After spending time raising money for political campaigns and realizing she didn't like fundraising, she took the advice of some friends and ran for state representative in the next primary election. As the Democratic candidate, she won by 61 percent of the vote.

With her political career up and running, Judy stayed in the house of representatives for 10 years and in her second term became the first woman to be elected to a leadership position.

"I was appointed to take a state senate seat in 1992 when the sitting state senator was elected to Congress," says Judy. "I ran for reelection in 1994, won, and stayed in the state senate until 1998. By that time I had been in the state legislature for 16 years."

In 1994, when Judy and Ben's grandson was born, Judy was on the ethics panel hearing cases in Columbus, Ohio.

"When Judy got the news of our grandson's birth, she was like a Scud missile aiming for Mount Sinai Hospital," says Ben.

"I took one look at that baby and my heart just flipped right over," remembers Judy. "That was a signal to me that I knew when to end my career. I had no doubt in my mind that I wanted to spend time with my grandchildren. When our daughter announced that she was going to have another baby, I decided I wasn't going to run for reelection again in 1998."

Although they are active grandparents, Ben and Judy still keep busy with their careers. Ben continues his lifelong career as an attorney and works with workmen's compensation and Social Security cases. Judy, although no longer in the state legislature, spends several days a month in Columbus as a member of the Ohio Election Commission.

As this North Olmsted couple reflects upon their 41-year marriage, they admit that they don't have a system or conscious plan for making their relationship work. What they attribute much of their marital success to is the balance they strike between their different personalities.

"Ben has a very low-key awareness of when to tread carefully with me and when to push a little," says Judy. "I have responded very well to that over the years. Ben has mellowed me, and I have given Ben a lot of excitement. We create a good balance."

"The thing I would say about Judy is that whenever we have quarrels, she doesn't carry a grudge," says Ben. "When it's over, it's over and I never hear about it again. She's pretty quick to forgive. I'm lucky to be married to a woman like her."

Another reason Ben is grateful for his wife is because of the support she gave him when his mother was dying. During the period when Ben's mother was ill, he put 15,000 miles on his car in seven months so that he could spend time with her.

"I was constantly back and forth between Cleveland and Endicott, New York," says Ben. "Judy never gave me a problem about it because she knew how much my mother meant to me."

"One thing I always liked about Ben was that he loved his mother and had a great deal of respect for her," says Judy.

One of the things Ben appreciates about Judy is that she gives him good advice.

"I regard Judy as my chief advisor," says Ben. "I respect her good intelligence. When I have a problem and talk to her about it, I would say I agree with her advice 95 percent of the time."

Judy smiles and says, "I'm trying to get it up to 99 percent."

Taking Those 12 Steps Together

NIKKI & HAROLD BABBIT

In the 1950s, American families gathered around the television set to watch the shows *Ozzie and Harriet, Leave It to Beaver,* and *Father Knows Best.* Viewers were riveted by what they saw because many of them lived a similar lifestyle—innocent, simple, and predictable.

With a home in the suburbs, a dog in the backyard, and an apron-clad mom in the kitchen, many families of the '50s were living an American dream. Nikki's family, on the other hand, was living an American nightmare.

"My growing-up years were rather unconventional for the '50s in that my mother struggled with alcoholism most of her life," explains Nikki. "I had a number of fathers as a result. By the time I was 18 years old, I had had five different last names."

At a time when teenage girls took turns hosting slumber parties for the purpose of painting toenails and trading movie magazines, Nikki couldn't even have friends drop by her house for a glass of lemonade.

"We were the family whose house kids weren't allowed to play at," she remembers.

So when Nikki sat next to Harold Babbit on their first date at the University of Iowa and watched a performance of *Long Day's*

Journey into Night, she wrestled with whether or not to tell him about her childhood.

"Seeing a play with a story line about addiction was very difficult for me because of what my upbringing had been like," explains Nikki. "I thought for sure that if Harold found out about my past, he would never want to see me again."

Nikki took a deep breath, felt the fear of rejection, and told Harold the truth about her background anyway.

"When she told me her story, I found it interesting, but because I didn't know anything about alcoholism or alcoholic families, I can't say that I had an emotional reaction to it," says Harold.

"What was endearing to me about Harold was that he was a wonderful listener and a natural nurturer," says Nikki.

Harold and Nikki were drawn to each other for opposite reasons. Nikki was attracted to Harold by his empathetic ear, even temperament, and ability to plan the future. Harold was attracted to Nikki's spontaneity and the ease with which she could communicate her feelings. Nikki made the perfect person for Harold to listen to, and Harold made the perfect person for Nikki to talk to. Like two puzzle pieces, they snapped together effortlessly.

Their attraction to one another quickly turned into a commitment that kept them close through life-changing decisions.

"After we graduated from college, Harold went to Columbia University with the idea that he wanted to become a college professor, and I went off to the Peace Corps," explains Nikki. "That summer, because I missed him greatly, and because some serious things were going on with my mom, I came home."

A year later, Harold decided to change his career path and study law at Yale University, but not before he proposed to Nikki on bended knee in his dorm room at Columbia.

In 1965, Nikki and Harold had what they considered to be a conventional Midwestern wedding. Two years later, they moved to Cleveland to start a family and create what they thought would be a conventional life in Shaker Heights, Ohio.

For the first 12 years the Babbits were in Cleveland, Nikki

taught high school at Hathaway Brown and University School, after which she earned a master's degree and Ph.D. and became a school psychologist. Her experience working with adolescents led her to become the founding director of New Directions, a residential and outpatient treatment facility for drug- and alcohol-dependent teenagers. Harold, in the meantime, was practicing public law as a partner at Calfee, Halter & Griswold and teaching public law at Cleveland Marshall Law School.

As working parents, this couple faced the normal challenges that parents face while raising three children, but none of those challenges put as much stress on their relationship as did Nikki's mother's addiction to alcohol.

"Dealing with my mother's alcoholic relapses and the new relationships she would get into became part of the rhythm of our family life," remembers Nikki. "When you have an alcoholic parent, it's typical for the issues to continue even when you leave home. One thing that helped keep our marriage strong was that Harold was a rock when it came to problems with my mother."

Having dealt with the disease of alcoholism for most of their marriage, however, did not prepare this couple for the day they learned their son had a drug and alcohol addiction.

"Finding out that our son was an alcoholic and drug addict definitely strained our relationship," says Nikki. "When a child uses drugs or alcohol, he or she works very hard at keeping it from the parents, so Harold and I were shocked when we learned about it. What added to the stress was that based on our different personalities, we had different ideas on what to do about the situation."

When their son's addiction was uncovered, Nikki and Harold became critical of exactly those personality traits in each other that they had fallen in love with when they first met.

"Throughout our marriage, Nikki had always commended me on being a rock," says Harold. "After we learned about our son's addiction, she complained about me not wanting to face the problem and talk about it. Conversely, whereas I had always been excited about the fact that she wore her feelings on her sleeve, I had become sick of hearing how she felt about our son's behavior."

Once their son began treatment for his drug addiction and alcoholism, Harold and Nikki began their own treatment program by attending a family week where they were taught the 12 steps of recovery.

"It was a very powerful family week," says Nikki, "and was a great wake-up call. People in recovery often say that you get kicked through the door in the beginning of treatment, but eventually feel gratitude for the 12-step program."

"Twelve-step recovery is a gift," says Harold. "Every person should have a chance to live that way, even if they have no connection to addictions."

Nikki feels that recovery not only strengthened her marriage and helped her son get sober and remain so for close to 20 years, it also made her more effective as executive director of New Directions, a position she retired from in 1995. As author of the book *Adolescent Drug & Alcohol Abuse—How to Spot It, Stop It, and Get Help for Your Family* (O'Reilly & Associates, 2000), Nikki currently teaches a weekly class at New Directions to educate parents of adolescent alcoholics and drug addicts.

"I was definitely a part of the fabric of the illness in that I grew up in an alcoholic home, but what strengthened my ability to understand parents of alcohol- and drug-addicted teenagers was the experience we had with our son," says Nikki.

By the time their son was well into recovery and their daughter, Jamie, was in college, Harold and Nikki were used to the twists and turns of their less than conventional lifestyle. So, when Jamie told them that she was a lesbian, they responded with nothing less than 100 percent acceptance and support.

"Jamie had not dated a lot in high school, but always had very close girlfriends," remembers Nikki. "She did date in college, but in her own awareness realized she was attracted to women."

When Nikki and Harold talk about their daughter's future, they do so with jubilance and anticipation.

"Jamie's partner, Andrea, who we call our daughter-in-law, wears an ancestral wedding ring that my grandmother gave me," says Nikki, "We hope to hear soon that Jamie is pregnant. They will be great parents."

Their daughter being a lesbian has not posed a problem for Harold and Nikki, but society's view of it has.

"What has been difficult is the fact that the world is cruel," says Nikki. "Because I do wear my feelings on my sleeve, I was much more vulnerable than Harold in the beginning. I would be in community meetings, and people would be saying things about gays and lesbians without realizing that what they were saying was very painful for me to hear."

Looking back, Nikki and Harold now understand that a foundation had been laid in both of their lives that would later allow them to freely embrace their daughter as a lesbian.

Whereas Harold grew up watching his aunt's family reject her for being a lesbian and having a 50-year relationship with a woman, Nikki experienced homosexuality in a more positive way.

"While I was growing up, my mother had a number of husbands," explains Nikki. "There was a friend of my mother's, who she didn't marry but who was a consistent father figure to me and stayed with us during the three times we moved. He in fact had similar characteristics to Harold in that he was very stable and was like a rock for our family.

"This man was gay. So, when I hear people say that gays and lesbians can't be parents, I do not understand. I had plenty of heterosexual fathers who came and went. Thank God I wasn't attracted to men like them."

Jamie Babbit, Harold and Nikki's second child, is now 33, living in Los Angeles, and is an established film and television director.

"Jamie has a high-profile career," says Nikki. "We're fortunate she is in the film community because it is very gay-friendly. We've met a lot of Jamie's friends who have told us that their parents don't support them in their choice to live how they were born. It's very sad to us because we are so proud of our daughter and very much support her."

When asked what commitment means in a marriage, Nikki refers to an enlightening piece of advice she once received. "Someone said to me years ago that marriage is all about 'learning' to love . . . what happens over time is that you learn what the components of love, like sacrifice and respect, are all about."

Believing that commitment takes work and does not occur naturally or magically, Harold views success in a marriage as being very much like success in a recovery program.

Simply stated, he says, "It works if you work it."

Acknowledgments

Throughout the process of writing this book, my husband, Dick Dawson, has given me unwavering support. I am grateful for his early-morning editing, but more importantly, for his 24-hour love.

To my two amazing teenage children, David and Katie, thank you for traveling with me on yet another book-writing journey. It wouldn't be the same without you.

Working with Caydie Heller has been an honor and a whole lot of fun. A gifted photographer, she caught the best in each couple and made this book come alive.

To Roger Heller, thank you for your professional advice, your common sense, and especially for your enthusiasm.

Much appreciation goes to Rosalie Wieder for editing this book. Your keen eye for detail has helped make the book the best it could be.

To David Gray, thank you for believing in this project. Your knowledge and expertise have been instrumental in the process.

In my quest to interview happily married couples, I was assisted by many people. I thank the following men and women for their encouragement and guidance, which led me to the couples whose stories I was meant to write:

Andrea Vecchio, David Budin, Barbara Rose, Mary Downey, Margaret Daykin, Andy Fishman, Karen Fuller, David Gray, Dianne Palmer, Sandra and Nate Bender, Sandy Vetrovsky, Brad Neary, Joy Resor, Vanessa Hagan, Chris Hagan, Tamar and Lenny Gray, Terri Moir, Mary Reynolds Powell and Doug Powell, Vic Voinovich, Caydie and Roger Heller, and Nina McClellan and Walter Nicholes.

Finally, I feel immense gratitude to all 40 couples who trusted me to tell their personal stories of love and commitment. Your courage, strength, and generosity will make a difference. Thank you for the privilege.

Photographer's Note

For me, this project quickly became more than a mere attempt to capture the images of 40 couples on black-and-white film. For a portrait photographer, the challenge lies in capturing the essence of a person without violating the space or psyche of that person. The tilt of a head, the clasping, touching, or holding of hands, tells much about a couple's relationship. In a photograph, the physical space between two people, juxtaposed with the closeness between them, speaks to me.

The photograph of each couple in this book is much more than a static rendering of two people. It is a living, loving illustration of the meeting and merging of two lives.

The willingness of these couples to share their voyage was truly a gift, and I am grateful to have had the opportunity to take part in the journey.

I would like to thank my husband, Roger, and children Jonathan, Cassidy, and Tessa for their encouragement, patience, and support. I would also like to thank Kathy Dawson, whose enthusiasm turned each experience into an exciting adventure.

About the Author

One of the Midwest's most well-known and respected relationship coaches, and founder of the Marriage Movement in Cleveland, Ohio, Kathy Dawson is a speaker and workshop leader, and the author of *Diagnosis: Married—How to Deal with Marital Conflict, Heal Your Relationship, and Create a Rewarding and Fulfilling Marriage* (Penguin Putnam/Perigee, 2000). Her experience as a weekly marriage/relationship columnist for Cleveland's *Plain Dealer* and her appearances on national and local television have made her an expert whose advice is widely sought. She lives in Cleveland Heights with her husband, Dick, her son, David, and her daughter, Katie.

Kathy Dawson would like to hear from you. If you're interested in receiving information about the Marriage Movement workshops or relationship coaching, or would like to invite Kathy Dawson to speak to your organization, contact:

The Marriage Movement
216-932-5016
e-mail: kd@marriagemovement.com
website: www.marriagemovement.com